# A History of the
# 17th Aero Squadron

*Our first Hun*

# A History of the
# 17th Aero Squadron

An American Squadron on the Western Front
During the First World War

Frederick Mortimer Clapp

LEONAUR

A History of the 17th Aero Squadron
An American Squadron on the Western Front During the First World War
by Frederick Mortimer Clapp

First published under the title
*A History of the 17th Aero Squadron*

Leonaur is an imprint of Oakpast Ltd

ISBN: 978-0-85706-635-0 (hardcover)
ISBN: 978-0-85706-636-7 (softcover)

http://www.leonaur.com

Publisher's Notes

The opinions of the authors represent a view of events in which he
was a participant related from his own perspective,
as such the text is relevant as an historical document.

The views expressed in this book are not necessarily
those of the publisher.

# Contents

## CONQUERORS

*Tribute? But what tribute to them can there be,*
*Now it is finished, now they are finished, and we*
*Have only now mere thoughts that stumble through mere words to*
*give*
*While, having had like us their lives to live.*
*They, in their self-effacing enterprise.*
*Over Flanders and its chill seas mist-hung.*
*Or over France, through hostile wind-swept skies—*
*They sought the fateful bullet made for them.*
*Their bullet destined how no man can tell*
*And seeking it, fearless, found it and so fell*
*Dead, but not conquered, out of the fight not won*
*Yet, and yet less bitter for their skill.*
*For their undying daring, less hard to win;*
*And so they measured finally their fears*
*And all the mortal dangers of their days*
*And made their high fate clean of all decays,*
*Supreme as was their readiness*
*And as their victory over self supreme.*
*Tribute of words? How poor to them would seem*
*Words, even words of deepest understanding*
*And how distasteful to them any tears!*

*Still, lest in reading after futile years*
*These pages along which their going has sown*
*The only glory this our tale can have—*
*Lest we should say, vanquished by life all unaware.*
*Trapped in mere living s pitfalls*
*Or basely by our very days undone.*
*Theirs was the only way and theirs the only peace,. . . .*
*Not then for their sake, but for our own.*
*Here are their names and dates,*
*Set like a gateway over the days and ways*

*In which they left us, passing on to where*
*No chance dark finger of a meaner hour*
*Can lay its sully on their memory now.*

*A gateway of their names—what tribute can there be*
*To them who gave Life life to make it free*
*Other than this or worthier or more proud?*
*Save this alone perhaps, if fate allow.*
*That, for their sake and for our own sake, we*
*Forget not, as their clear eyes saw, to see*
*Steadfastly their victory victoriously*
*In ways that they would not condemn.*
*What more? What more could be?*
*There is no other tribute we can pay to them!*

*Nil actum reputans si quid superesset agendum*

December 1918

# Flying Officers Killed in Action

—

| | |
|---|---|
| 1st Lieut. George P. Glenn | July 20, 1918 |
| 1st Lieut. Murray K. Spidle | August 4, 1918 |
| 1st Lieut. Ralph D. Gracie | August 12, 1918 |
| 1st Lieut. Lyman E. Case | August 14, 1918 |
| 2nd Lieut. William H. Shearman | August 14, 1918 |
| 1st Lieut. Merton L. Campbell | August 23, 1918 |
| 1st Lieut. Lloyd A. Hamilton | August 24, 1918 |
| 1st Lieut. Lawrence Roberts | August 26, 1918 |
| 2nd Lieut. Howard P. Bittinger | August 26, 1918 |
| 2nd Lieut. Harry H. Jackson, Jr. | August 26, 1918 |
| 2nd Lieut. Gerald P. Thomas | September 22, 1918 |
| 1st Lieut. Harold G. Shoemaker | October 6, 1918 |
| 1st Lieut. Glenn D. Wicks | October 6, 1918 |

CHAPTER 1[1]

# Organization and Training

The 17th Aero Squadron came into being at the beginning of what is now known as the Air Service, on May 13, 1917, a month after war was formally declared by the United States. At that time it was called Company "M," later Company "B." Still later it became the 29th Provisional Aero Squadron, Aviation Section, Signal Corps, and then the 17th. Its entire enlisted personnel were volunteers, and a majority of them had "come in" believing—the idea was sown broadcast by recruiting sergeants in various parts of the country—that they were to be eventually, not mechanics, but flying officers.

They came from thirty-five states of the Union, from Porto Rico, Canada, and Mexico, and they were among the first to arrive at Kelly Field, San Antonio, Texas—an aerodrome which was, at that moment, rather a project than a reality.

The squadron's experience at Kelly Field was, in many respects, an augury of its future for, from that time on, it was always to be the first to try, or have "tried upon it," the experiments to which a new service inevitably gives rise. It was the first squadron sent to Canada to be trained by the British; the first squadron to go back to the fields near Fort Worth that were to be administered by British and American officers working together; the first completely trained squadron to be sent overseas with its complete quota of pilots; the first squadron to be attached to British squadrons at the front (and therefore the first in the battle line); and the first squadron to be equipped by the British and brigaded with them, in active service, under their command.

Having been the first to carry out these experiments, as well as

1. The material contained in this chapter is due to the kindness of Lieut. David T. Wells, from whose first sketch of it the general sequence of the narrative and some of the wording have been retained.

others on which no stress need now be laid, it suffered all the handicaps which the objects of experiment commonly suffer. And the fact that the 17th Squadron finally proved itself so efficient and retained, to such a degree, its *esprit de corps*, when at last it began to take part, as a unit, in operations at the front, speaks volumes for the character of those first volunteers. It speaks volumes too for their cheerful loyalty that, without rancour or bitterness, they "carried on"—false as had been the ideas given them of what their duties were to be—when in France their friends, who enlisted later than they, turned up as pilots while they remained mechanics.

The credit for the record of a scout squadron naturally goes to the flying officers who have taken the risks and done the fighting, but no small part of it should go to the enlisted men, who have to be untiringly on the lookout for loose wires and hidden broken parts; who, in busy times, work all night long to have machines ready for a patrol at dawn; and who at best can have only the satisfaction that comes from making possible the deeds of other men. What pilots and enlisted men, working together in a spirit of conscious self-sacrifice, can do in spite of repeated discouragement, is made evident by this letter from Lieut. Gen. J. M. Salmond, G.O.C., R.A.F., to Gen. M. M. Patrick, Chief of the Air Service:

Dear General Patrick:
Now that the time has come when Nos. 17 and 148 Squadrons return to you, I wish to say how magnificently they have carried out their duties during the time they have been lent to the British Aviation.
Every call has been answered by them to the highest degree, and when they have arrived with you, you will have two highly efficient squadrons filled with the offensive spirit.
I should like to recommend, if you agree, that they be fitted with S. E. 5 machines. Their formation flying is good and I consider this type of machine would suit them.
Yours sincerely,
(Sgd.) J. M. Salmond.

The results of the unconquerable determination to do their best that called forth General Salmond's letter are shown with still greater force by the following facts, which give, in two words so to speak, the record of the 17th Squadron as a fighting unit for the period July 15—October 28. During fifty-one days on which we sent out offensive patrols over the lines, we destroyed and had confirmed fifty-four enemy machines and balloons and drove down out of control ten more, or in all a total of sixty-four. In other words, we destroyed or drove down 1.25½ enemy aircraft for every fighting day of our active operations. For the same period we dropped from low altitudes, on hostile transport and infantry, 1,164 bombs and fired into them 31,806 rounds.[2]

To get, however, an adequate idea of the squadron's career as a whole, we must go back briefly over its history before it became a force with which the Hun had so considerably to reckon.

Its life began, as we have said, at Kelly Field. There its work consisted chiefly of drills and fatigues. The men surveyed and built the first sewerage and water system, and the first barracks and hangars of the camp. On August 2, 1917, with the third commanding officer assigned to it within three months, Lieut. Robert Oldys, the squadron moved to Toronto, Canada. In July a reciprocal agreement had been made by the British and American governments under the terms of which the British were to organize and train, at the Royal Flying Corps' camps in and about Toronto, the pilots and mechanics of ten squadrons for Overseas service. A certain number of American cadets were already in training at these camps. The 17th Squadron was the first group of enlisted men to arrive in fulfilment of the terms of the agreement with regard to personnel.

On its arrival, on August 4th, it was sent to Recruits' Depot, at Leaside. There the men were given three weeks' British drill and discipline. They "formed fours" and they "stood at ease." Then they were split up into detachments and sent on to various other camps for training in rigging and fitting and all the trades involved in the repair and upkeep of aeroplanes. The gunners and wireless operators, for example, went to the school of Military Aeronautics, at Toronto University; six men went to the Motor Transport Depot, Toronto, of which they afterwards had charge; seventy-five men went to the Royal Flying Corps Aeroplane Repair Park; six others, to the flying field at Desoronto; and ninety-nine men were left at Leaside. The C. O. and Headquarter's staff moved to Camp Borden, one hundred miles away, to take charge of other Americans who, in the meantime, had arrived there.

It is hard to hold an organization together under such circum-

2. For full statistical record of the 17th Squadron, as a fighting unit, see Chapter 7, parts 1, 2 and 3.

stances; but the men were apparently eager to learn, for the wireless operators and gunners soon became instructors of cadets, while thirteen of the N. C. O.'s who had remained at Leaside were put in charge of Recruits' Depot when the N. C. O.'s of the Royal Flying Corps detachment there were given leave.

But if it is difficult to keep an organization alive when its personnel has been broken up into scattered groups, it is still more difficult to work up an *esprit de corps* under conditions such as these. The men were really civilians in uniform, and not too well disciplined either. When the squadron reassembled at Leaside before proceeding to Texas, it was given the task of washing the station mascots—"Bruno," a large woolly dog, and a goat named "Billy." The result was that " Bruno" turned up the next morning with a perfectly clean shave, while "Billy" ambled out into the world with a large "U. S." painted on his side, and with a long streamer tied to his tail bearing the legend: "17th Aero Squadron." He was also noticeably the worse for drink, and when in the rain the men marched off to the train, "Billy" had such a headache that he was only too glad to see them go. The squadron left Toronto on October 12th, under the command of Major Geoffrey H. Bonnell, and proceeded to Fort Worth, Texas. An advance party of twenty men had left for the same destination on September 24th.

The general direction of training in Canada and at the new fields near Fort Worth was in the hands of Brig. General Hoare, R. F. C. The officers who commanded the American troops stationed in and about Toronto had been, first Major Shepler A. Fitzgerald, then Capt. (afterwards Lieut. Col.) David L. Roscoe.

Major Bonnell was an American who had been a flight commander in the R. F. C. and afterwards C. O. of the 79th Canadian Training Squadron. His staff in the 17th was made up of the following ground officers: Lieut. H. McC. Bangs, adjutant; Lieut. David T. Wells, supply officer; 2nd Lieut. Howard B. Hull, gunnery officer; and 2nd Lieut. Ellsworth C. Goldsworthy, R. F. C., liaison officer. Eight cadets who had finished their training were attached to the squadron and proceeded with it to Texas: Walter A. Jones, Ralph D. Gracie, Orville A. Ralston, Charles W. France, Ralph W. Snoke, Oliver P. Johnson, Harold G. Shoemaker, Jesse O. Creech.

Of the latter, all but one finally received their commissions and came overseas with the squadron. Jones was killed in the first fatal flying accident that occurred after our arrival in Texas.

Our destination was Hicks, a small station near Fort Worth, which was afterwards called Taliaferro Field, No. 1. The aerodrome there was in a deplorably unfinished state. Barracks for the men and hangars there were, near enough completion to be serviceable, but the officers lived in tents from which they had to chase an occasional tarantula. There were no telephones and practically no transport. The aeroplanes destined for our use were still in their long wooden boxes, and stores were only just beginning to arrive.

We began work however in earnest and at once. Flights were formed as completely as the officers' imperfect knowledge of their men's capacity permitted. Sgts. Hayes R. Miller, John B. Douglass, Lomas Gipner, and Cameron A. Smith were put in charge of them and Edward C. Bauer was made first sergeant. On the second day after our arrival the first machine was in the air. Within a week all machines assigned to us had been unpacked, erected, and were flying. Cadets W. A. Jones, R. D. Gracie, and O. P. Johnson were made flight commanders. They worked hard and well. They showed undeniable ability and, for months before they received their commissions, they did in a creditable manner the work of officers.

New cadets, who came to the field to finish their training, were taught further details of the art of flying by cadets who had already really learned to fly. We messed where and how we could, and the cadets get a certain amusement of their own by having such a series of forced landings, in the neighbourhood of a girls' school not many miles away, that all engine trouble came to be looked upon with suspicion. But our earnestness was undeniable and, for the most part, officers, cadets, and men were full of a happy adventurous spirit inspired by the oft-repeated promise that the 17th was to be the first American pursuit squadron to reach the front.

By November 1st, thirty cadets had completed their training; most of them had also received their commissions; the enlisted personnel had become a fairly smooth-running organization; and the squadron's equipment for overseas service was as complete as it could be made without supply tables. For the period of our training at Hicks we held the flying record for the field—sixty-three hours a day on seven machines serviceable. Just before we were due to entrain for the port of embarkation. Major Bonnell, who had also been in temporary command of the post, was relieved from duty with the squadron, by Major Martin F. Scanlon—our sixth commanding officer in ten months. Lieutenant Hull was also relieved at the same time, as gunnery officer, by Lieut. Arthur B. Lapsley.

When the squadron arrived at Garden City (December 23), it found New York in the grip of a coal famine and the longest cold snap the city had known for years. Sailing was held up for nearly a fortnight, and during the interval commissions arrived for those cadets who had not yet received them. The passenger list had, however, already been made up and, on board the transport, these the latest of our officers had to put up with accommodations meant for sergeants.

We sailed finally on January 9th on the *Carmania*—one of a convoy of fourteen ships. Everything went according to schedule and we arrived in Liverpool on January 25th. The voyage was a normal wartime crossing—no very rough, no very pleasant weather, many rumours, but no submarines. From Liverpool we went to the American "Rest Camp" at Romsey, and there, so far as discomfort went, we got our first taste of what war is. It was really more than a taste. Not many weeks later the squadron took part in the British retreat of March and April and, as a fighting unit, the men were with the British during their advance of September and October; but in all their incessant moving back and forth through the mud and confusion of twice and thrice fought-over territory, never were they so uncomfortable as at this "Rest Camp."

And they had other new reasons for being disheartened, if anything could have disheartened them. They had been told, as we have said, that the 17th was to be the first pursuit squadron overseas; they were well trained and organized; they were eager to do their part in the struggle; and yet it was now proposed to split the squadron up again—for reasons no one could fathom—and scatter the men among the Royal Flying Corps training camps in England. In the end, however, that blow too was averted, and the squadron was sent to the front to learn how to rig S. E. 5's and take care of Hispano-Suiza engines. For this purpose it was arranged that each flight, under the command of a ground officer, should be attached to a separate R. F. C. fighting squadron for duty and final training, while the C. O. and the pilots went to various flying schools in Great Britain for instruction on war machines. Lieutenant Bangs took Headquarters flight; Lieutenant Lapsley, "A" flight; Lieutenant Wells, "B" flight; Lieutenant James G. Bennett, a flying officer, who volunteered to help out in the hope of getting his higher training at the front, took "C" flight.

On February 9th the squadron sailed from Southampton for Havre, with a shipload of mules and horses destined for the use of a Jewish regiment on its way to Palestine. A Donegal Irishman, one of the

"Old Contemptibles," with two wound stripes and two decorations, had charge of this strange consignment, and the amusement he displayed at the nature of his command was quite unbounded.

At Havre Captain Stradling, D. A. A. G. of the British armies, met us when we disembarked. He had been sent down from G. H. Q., R. F. C, to see the flights off to their various destinations. D. A. A. G., by the way, for the benefit of those who never learned or have now forgotten the shorthand of the war, stands for Deputy Assistant Adjutant General. Headquarters flight was assigned to 24 Squadron, at Martigny; "A" flight to 84 Squadron, at Guizancourt; "B" to 60 Squadron, at Ste. Marie Cappell, near Hazebrouck, on the Flanders front; and "C" to 56 Squadron, at Baizieux. All left at once except "B" flight which followed the next day.

Up to the beginning of the German "push," on March 21st, all of the flights had much the same experience. To put part of a unit of one nationality into a squadron of another, without causing friction, requires from both the greatest tact. In our case the arrangement was that instruction was to be entirely in British hands, but discipline in those of the respective American officers in charge.

Before long our men knew their machines and engines well enough to be rather a help than a hindrance to the squadrons to which they were attached. And they made rapid progress, because for the most part both officers and men realized that they were part of an experiment in training squadrons in the field, and that, upon their ability to get on well with the British, the future of this method of training in no small measure depended. How well they understood the situation is made apparent by the fact that, in nearly five months, during which they were attached to British squadrons, no really unpleasant incident arose between the two nationalities.

The 17th Squadron, it must be remembered, was handicapped in many ways by its complete detachment from the American service. More than that, during our first months in France, the flights were totally out of touch with one another. Later on a succession of officers, chosen it seemed quite at random and placed in command of American Aviation Units with the British, came for a casual hour or two, at widely scattered intervals, to see how we were "getting on." This, however, was long after our detachments had, each with its British unit, settled down to serious war work. The Air Service apparently forgot that we existed. Supplies, particularly clothing, were unobtainable. The squadron was destitute of transport.

When the German drive began all flights, with the exception of "B," were still on the aerodromes to which they had been sent originally. "B" flight, however, had moved to Bailleul where it had had its baptism of shell fire, shrapnel, and bombing, through which it had come unscathed. A little later (March 23rd) it moved to Bellevue, back of Arras. The whole squadron was now on the front involved in the Hun attack and, from the end of March on, all flights took part in a succession of movements carried out in the face of the enemy advance. They helped build new aerodromes; they helped abandon them and build still others as the British army moved back.

Since the 17th Squadron was one of the very few American units that saw from the inside this great cycle of movements, the changes of station made by its scattered flights are not without interest. Headquarters flight began its retreat on the first day of the drive (March 21st) when 24 Squadron, R. A. F., left Moreuil. It abandoned the aerodrome only a few hours before the Hun reached it, and some of our men were among those who remained to burn, if necessary, the hangars and quarters. Before their task was finished, the Hun had all but come across the other side of the field and they were under machine gun fire. From Moreuil the flight went with 24 Squadron to Bertangles; then from Bertangles to Conteville.

At Guizancourt "A" flight had been under artillery fire, while with 84 Squadron, R. A. F., before, they moved to Roye; and the last man to leave got away only an hour and a half before the Germans came up. From Roye it went to Vert-Galand Farm (March 24th) and then to Maison-Ponthieu (March 29th). At last the Hun was held and "A" flight made with 84 Squadron only one more move (April 5th) before the 17th was reassembled—this time to Bertangles. The other two flights made many similar changes of station. "B" flight had come down from Flanders to Bellevue with 60 Squadron just in time to stand by to move.

All the British squadron's stores and property were divided up so that, if need arose, they could be destroyed in the order of their relative importance. Nothing, however, in spite of much foreboding, was lost in moving to Fienvillers (March 28th). There "B" flight remained until April when it went to a field not far from Rougefay (April 12th), which was the last camp it occupied as a detached flight with 60 Squadron. "C" flight moved once (March 26th) from Baizieux to Valheureux Farm, near Candas.

These Spring months were one of the busiest and most exciting times the R. A. F. had ever known and, during them, the enlisted men of the 17th Squadron learned much more than the mere care of their machines. They knew now what it meant to send out patrols and move incessantly from one aerodrome to another at the same time. And that knowledge gained in actual experience was, if possible, even more valuable to them than the knowledge they gained of service machines and engines. Later, when they were operating as an American unit with the R. A. F., word came in the middle of the night to move in five hours, and they were ready before that brief interval had passed.

On April 1st. Headquarters flight was detached from 24 Squadron and until May 20th it worked as a salvage section under the 22nd Wing, R. A. F. In those five weeks it salvaged twenty-five enemy machines and fourteen British, chiefly without lights in the darkness of the night, within five hundred yards of the German lines.

During the latter part of those anxious months, and in the months of May and June, other American squadrons followed the trail blazed by the 17th. Other officers were placed successively in command of the American squadrons with the B. E. F., and still there appeared to be little hope that our flights would be reformed and put into active operations. By the end of May the enlisted men had been in training for eighteen months; they had been four months at the front; and yet they seemed as far as ever from the realization of their ambition of operating as an American unit. They had had special training on the rigging and engines of English 200 h. p., French 220 h. p., and Viper Hispano-Suiza S. E. 5's, and now it suddenly transpired—who was responsible, we wondered, for this lack of foresight?—that England could spare no machines of that type.

On May 18th Major Harold Fowler, M. C, succeeded Major Thomas S. Bowen and, soon after he assumed command of the American Air Service Units with the British Armies, it was decided that the 17th should be put on 110 h. p. Le Rhone Sopwith Camels. The mechanics were given a month to master their overhaul and upkeep—machines and engines. Headquarters and "A" flights went on May 20th for that purpose to 23 Squadron and then to 80 Squadron; "B" flight was assigned to 46 and "C" flight to 3 Squadron, R. A. F. The men learned rapidly. On June 20th all four flights were sent to a field at Petite Synthe, near Dunkirk, to become once more a unit and resume their identity as a squadron.

At last we, who had been ready so long—at last we were going to take a real part in the fighting which for nearly six months we had heard and seen, but into which we had not yet been able to put—so slowly, so feebly and heedlessly, do the wheels of administration often grind—had not, one might more accurately say, been allowed to throw our whole strength.

Lieutenant Lapsley had, in the meantime, been relieved, on admission to hospital, by 1st Lieut. Lorenz K. Ayres as armament officer, and Lieutenant Bangs was replaced, as adjutant, by 1st Lieut. Frederick Mortimer Clapp, formerly adjutant of the 22nd Aero Squadron.

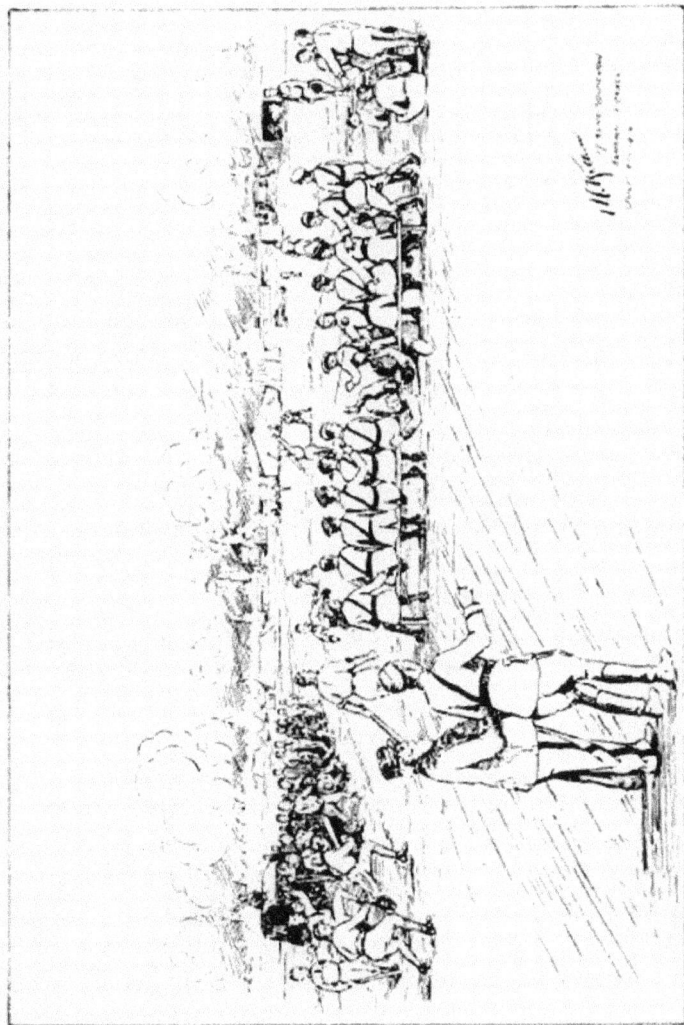

Fourth of July, 1918.   A foul tip fouls Robert Lorraine

# CHAPTER 2

# The Dunkirk Front

Our new C.O., who had received his orders far South, at the other end of the line, and had flown up from Dijon through the rain to assume the command that he held through all our active operations, was 1st Lieut., (now Major) Samuel B. Eckert, formerly CO. of the 9th Aero Squadron. Like all our pilots, ground officers, and enlisted personnel, he was British trained. He had flown at London Colney, Turnberry, and Ayr. At the Front he had been on S. E. 5's with 84 Squadron, R.A.F., at Bertangles, and with 80 Squadron, R.A.F., on Camels, at Château Thierry during some of the fiercest and most decisive fighting of the "push."

Our senior flight commander, 1st Lieut., (now Major) Morton L. Newhall, or as we knew him "Mort," had flown on offensive patrol, on S.E.5's and Camels with 3 and 84 Squadrons, R.A.F. Shortly after we arrived at Petite Synthe, he was put in command of the 148th Aero Squadron which, flying officers and men, was also British trained and was being reassembled and reorganized (July 1st) not far from us, on the other side of the canal at Cappelle Aerodrome. Mort's new dignity meant a great loss to us. He left us taking with him the marvellous pup, his inseparable "Shadow," and leaving in us a void filled happily however with a sense that his success was sure. And we were not mistaken. Rarely has a commanding officer shown himself so wise, so modest, and so intelligently sympathetic, rarely has he won so completely and kept so securely at once the deep respect and the warm admiration both of his pilots and subordinates.

The 148th were equipped with Clerget Camels and like us operated with the 65th Wing, R.A.F. Our relations with them were always delightfully fraternal. We called each other up and inquired what each other's patrols had seen and done and what the activity on the lines was like. They dined us and we dined them. We took counsel together, and their fine record was a matter of joy to us as we watched it grow.

Lieutenant Tipton was promoted to be "B" flight commander. He had served with 3 Squadron, R.A.F., and had a remarkable knowledge of aeroplane engines. "C" flight was commanded by 1st Lieut. Lloyd A. Hamilton whose record while flying with 3 Squadron, R.A.F., was four and a quarter enemy aeroplanes and balloons destroyed, 1st Lieut. Weston W. Goodnow was given command of "A" flight. He had acquired his background of experience at the Front with No. 203 British Squadron, as had Lieutenants Frost and Campbell theirs with 209 and 54 Squadrons respectively. Lieutenants Desson, Dixon, and Gracie had seen service with 209 Squadron, R.A.F., on Camels, and Lieutenant Williams had been with 3 Squadron, R.A.F., although he had never crossed the lines. The remainder of our original pilots came to us from the Training Brigade through the pool from which all British trained pilots were drawn.

That background, that common experience, was an immense asset. Each of our pilots had ideas of his own, gained in actual fighting, about the way to carry out offensive patrols. Every detail of the operation of a Le Rhone engine or the use of aeroplane controls in flying formation or fighting was made the subject of heated discussions in which many ideas—based upon the long, thorough, and often painful experience of the British—came to light and became part and parcel of our general knowledge of organization and tactics.

Nor was that all. We profited even more directly by many details of British system. Was it not laid down, for example, in their regulations that no pilot was to cross the lines until he had been three weeks in France and, in addition to showing marked proficiency in flying and manoeuvring, had flown a certain number of hours on line patrol and had fired successfully a certain number of rounds from the air at a fixed target? The British never sent a pilot straight into the fray, raw from training fields. That mere detail of administration and foresight saved them and us many lives and prevented disasters from happening, at the very beginning of the squadron's career, that would have permanently lamed its offensive spirit.

Major Harold Fowler, who was in a way our American Wing Commander, was also British trained. His past experience with the Royal Flying Corps included many kinds of machines, from artillery observation two-seaters to Camels, and he had fought and flown, from the outbreak of the war, not only in France but in East Africa.

He therefore understood better than many Americans the possibilities and the difficulties of British organization; he saw, as no one before him had in the slightest degree tried to see, the necessity of seconding us in the desire we entertained of making our relations with the British happy and friendly. He had his own particular Camel which, with that of Col. J. A. Cunningham, D. F. C. (O. C. 65th Wing, R.A.F.), was kept in our hangars and, from the beginning of our activity, he was a not infrequent visitor at Petite Synthe. After we moved to Auxi-le-Château, he moved his Armstrong hut and had it set up in our woods, and when he was not visiting the 148th, or G.H.Q., R.A.F., or his own headquarters at Montreuil-sur-Mer, he ate and lodged with us.

After all our "busses" had been collected from Marquise and properly tuned up, after we had made numerous practice formation flights, and had fired, early and late, at the aeroplane target, in the marsh, by the dunes of St. Pol-sur-Mer, till there was nothing left of it but shreds, we were ready for line patrols of which we did, before going into active offensive work, 188 hours, sending out in all 114 machines. It was on starting out upon these that we received our official secret insignia, a white dumb-bell painted on each side of the fuselage aft of the cockpit. The 148th fought under the sign of the "White Triangle." Later, in contemplation of our return to the American Armies, we adopted and had confirmed as our own symbol, "The Great Snow Owl," of which Sgt. Hayden C. Kellum made a forceful sketch. But it was with the "Dumb-Bell" on our sides that we fought all our battles, and the other more decorative emblem can never quite replace it or have for us the same fullness of significance.

The field at Petite Synthe, near Dunkirk, lies in a rough triangle between the main railway line from Dunkirk to Calais, the by-road running from Petite Synthe to Pont de Petite Synthe on the Bourbourg Canal, and the sidings of the railway on which hospital trains belonging to the French Medical Corps were drawn up waiting for sudden calls from this or that part of the front. The by-road crosses the field on its south-western side. This was one of the oldest aerodromes in French Flanders and belonged, in the beginning, to the Royal Naval Air Service. It had been the home of some great British Squadrons of the 5th Wing, R.N.A.S.: among them, the 2nd, 5th, 6th, 11th, afterwards the 202nd, 205th, 206th, and 211th, Royal Air Force, as well as the 49th R.F.C., the 87th, R.A.F., and the 85th R.A.F., which the great Canadian scout pilot, Major Bishop, commanded.

The land round about is flat and often, in the morning and evening, full of ground mist. The weather too is full of the changeableness of a sea-coast country. Beautiful long lines of poplars border the by-road and the Route Nationale to Calais. From the air the country looks like an immense irregular patchwork of light and dark green, interspersed with the gray and brown of well-tilled fields, from which stand out the spire of St. Eloi at Dunkirk, not far from the city's network of docks and shipbuilding yards, and, to the East, the many-moated, star-shaped and battered Nieuport, on the Yser Canal.

The squadrons that occupied the field—there were almost always three of them—were housed in wooden huts, arranged inside for the hammocks of the "ratings" of the Royal Naval Air Service. Outside they were banked with revetments of sandbags and each squadron had its own dugout which, in the case of the old 202nd, afterward Major Bishop's and then ours, was a vast structure like an oblong, broken-down step pyramid, in the making of which nearly thirty thousand sandbags had been used. You needed dugouts in that region, for the Hun came over, and often in force, every clear night. You watched the sky in the evening and, if a star came out as it grew dark, you were sure to hear someone remark: "Well, I guess old Jerry will be over tonight." The strictest rules were enforced with regard to lights and when the siren at Dunkirk, familiarly called "Mournful," bellowed, to be answered shrilly by Coudekerque and St. Pol-sur-Mer, the dynamo in the workshop lorry came to a dead stop.

The Hun sailed over black spaces. There was not a gleam or glimmer in the plains. But around his droning Gothas, the pulsation of which you came quickly enough to distinguish from the hum of Handley Pages, F.E.'s or night-scouting Camels, the black of the sky was full of innumerable winking stars of "Archy" and the rumble of the barrage. The Hun only "got something" near us twice at Dunkirk—once when he put a bomb on the aerodrome side of the hospital trains and blew all their glass out, and once, the night we arrived, when he dropped a large one on the French Cavalry shack behind our Mess, leaving a deep hole in the mud and much match-wood. The chief effect of this attack upon the squadron was to make some of us bolt out of our quarters in pyjamas.

Most of the men seemed to like bomb raids, although some of them felt happier when they were standing around, joking about "Jerry," within diving distance of the mouth of the dugout. They looked upon raids as a spectacle not to be missed. The personnel of the French hospital trains were less devoted to fireworks for their own sake. They

25

GRAND STAND SEATS ON THE DUGOUT OF PETIT SYNTHE

had perhaps had too much of them in four long years. At all events, on clear nights—and there were many during the first part of our stay in those much-bombed regions—you would find the whole French force of the neighbourhood packed in the inner stifling darkness of the dugout, into which the roar of anti-aircraft fire and the crashing "*zong*" of bombs came muted, while the whole American force conspicuously displayed itself on the roof, using it as if it were the grandstand at Paine's Pyrotechnics.

In a shack on the by-road, near the ditch where fat rats lived, we set up our Officers' Mess. We believed in making it as comfortable as possible; and anyone surprising us between patrols in those first weeks would have seen pilots and commanding officer standing on trestle-tables or piled gasoline boxes, painting the ceiling of the shack white and the little beams a pale green, or busily laying old canvas on the rough floor. They did not despise comfort and some touch of beauty. They came in from fighting the Hun to roll the tennis court—an operation that consisted in dragging an old cement beam behind a Fiat truck round and round in the mud in front of the Mess. Todd and Case and Desson, and sometimes even three or four others, managed to squat or stand tottering on the twisting beam to give it greater weight, while "Army," as Armstrong was familiarly called, "chauffed" the truck.

There were hurried trips to Calais for added luxuries. All the light-green iron garden chairs the Nouvelles Gaieties of that place possessed were bought and brought home. Wicker chairs and cushions were bought too. *Gravures galantes*—but not too "*galantes*"—as well as perfectly proper prints in colour of "*Les Noces Alsaciennes*" were tacked on the wall. A piano was hired, and a gramophone, with a couple of dozen records chiefly of semi-classical music, such as "*Asa's Death*" by Grieg or the "*Song of the Boatmen on the Volga*," was squeezed out of the Red Cross. We also designed and had executed by Day, the sailmaker, drop-lights, the stand of which was made of an empty *soixante-quinze* shell-case, well polished, and the shade of a yellow silk edged with beads and surmounted by a shining nose-piece.

There were unwritten rules of the Mess. One had to be more or less dressed for dinner; one had to come up to the CO. and formally apologize if one were late; one did not begin one's soup until he did; one did not light a cigar or cigarette until he had lighted his. We never wore Sam Browne belts at dinner, but the Officer of the Day wore his belt at all times. No excuse was valid for breaking any of these rules, or by speech or act disturbing the decorum of the Mess. Not that we were quiet or gloomy. Far from it! We soothed our digestion with laughter and endless poking of fun at one another. And nothing brought forth such peals of merriment as the infraction, through thoughtlessness, of any of our rules. The offender bought drinks or cigars or both all around, depending upon the gravity of his crime, to shouts of "Randolph, Randolph, take an order!"

Those were also the days when the Pilots' Room was worked out in the C.O.'s canvas hut, various partitions of which were occupied by the "Staff." Maps were feverishly pasted together by the force of the Squadron Office until they covered the walls; the "line" was drawn in blue pencil upon them with anxious attention to accuracy; data technical and confidential about operations and flying, that flowed in copiously from 65th Wing Headquarters, were made accessible. There the C.O. and the pilots met to discuss "shows." There the colonel, the wing adjutant, the wing equipment officer, the wing armament officer, and the dignitaries of the brigade were received. They came frequently and without formality, easy and charming and deeply interested in our progress. We had only to ask to receive, within reason. They did everything in their power to help and enlighten, putting their experience freely at our disposal.

The air was always full of the roar of engines on a fair day, and even on days when mists hung about the plains or clouds rolled up from the south and west, there was a roar at least from the test bench. We watched the big bombing formations of the 211th take off" in front of the hangars—twelve, fourteen, even sixteen D.H.9's getting away, one after the other, and disappearing into the haze toward Calais to get their height. When we escorted them on their long trip to Bruges Docks, which they bombed twice a day regularly for weeks, we had a sense of personal interest in their going; for were not our orders to meet them at 15,000 feet over Dunkirk at a given moment? We kept a weather eye on our squadron clock and thirty-five minutes after the last D.H.9 had thundered away, we "got off" taking great pride in leaving the ground information, one flight after another, and returning "wing tip to wing tip" in one solid *buzz*.

We set up an engine shop, carpenter's shop, tinsmith's shop, sailmaker's shop, Q.M. and technical stores, armoury and canteen, mostly out of dilapidated huts or old aeroplane boxes and bits of salvaged canvas. We strung telephone and electric light wires; we filled in roads; we found pieces of burlap with which to blind the windows against the night–flying Hun. Headquarters flight with its engine repair, its supplies, its parked lorries and tenders, its hum of saws and drills, its hammer and bang of the blacksmith shop, was organized and speeded up.

The Chinese, who worked on the revetting of the shacks and had long ago camouflaged the hangars with strange characters of their own, watched our activities with smiles and curiosity. At evening through the mist we saw still other companies of them trooping along the road to their camp by the canal, coming home on a train we called the "Chinks' Limited" that drew up puffing and full of them on a siding behind our shacks.

It was upon the organization of the flights, shops, and stores that most, perhaps, depended in this formative period. Happily few mistakes were made. Lieutenant Wells had been so many months with the squadron that he knew the character and ability of most of the enlisted men. Sgt., afterward M.S.E. John B. Douglass, seconded by Sgt. Hayes R. Miller, was placed in charge of the technical side of aeroplanes and engine upkeep and overhaul. His work corresponded to that of the technical sergeant major in an English squadron or to the engineering officer of an American unit. His responsibilities were great and he met them unfailingly.

Sgt. Clay A. Wellborn was made Truckmaster and had under his supervision the entire equipment of R. A. F. transport allotted to us, that consisted of one Crossley touring car, seven Leyland lorries, five Crossley tenders, two work- shop lorries, six trailers, two water-trailers, four motorcycle side-cars, eight motorcycles, as well as the five Fiat trucks with four trailers, a large water-trailer, one Harley-Davidson side-car and one Cadillac which, before we reached Petite Synthe, had been put upon our charge by the Services of Supply of the American Air Service. He succeeded admirably and was soon made First Sergeant, a berth that Sgt. Lomas Gipner had filled during our first weeks of reorganization. Sgt. Eldon E. Hively was given charge of "A" flight, Sgt. Devillo Sloan, who was later nominated for training as a flyer, was given charge of "B" flight, Sgt. C. A. Smith of "C" flight, in each case carrying on the work that they had begun in Texas.

Repairs were done under pressure. But any machine seriously crashed was at once returned to No. 8 Aircraft Park and from the Depot a new machine was delivered to us immediately. It was a matter of hours only before we had "written off" the wreck and taken the new "bus" on to our strength. A "Casualty Report" went to the Wing by dispatch rider and a "signal" came back, for example: "Sopwith Camel D 4598 struck off strength 17th Aero Squadron. One Sopwith Le Rhone Camel allotted, 1 A.D. Please collect." And the CO. would say: "Todd, will you get this bus?" handing him the signal. We were liable to be "straffed" if our "Casualty Report" was even a little late.

The same was true of transport and supplies, with almost no exception, from tools to sandbags, from acetone to rivets and flashlights. But there was no promiscuous and wholesale dumping of material on our charge. The British had too much use for everything a squadron needs. They were short—sometimes in some things anxiously short. You had to give chapter and verse, in proper form, as tersely as possible, for all your requisitions. You had your fortnightly allowance of each item; you had your mobilization tables for every "spare." But what you could show a real need for you got. That was where the functioning of the Supply Office, or Equipment Office as it was called, came in. It was admirably run under Lieut. David T. Wells's direction by Sgt. Cecil N. Douglass.

Had it been in doubt of its procedure or its rights, had it hesitated or failed to "indent" when the appointed moment came for routine supplies, we should have been handicapped. It didn't. Rare occasions excepted it functioned with a smoothness that brought expressions of admiration from the British, who are generally slow to praise. Moments there were when a rebuilt engine could not be made serviceable on the appointed day, because a special part was not obtainable— such as, for example, the notorious small reamers and metric gauges that we worried about for more than a week.

Forty-eight engines were rebuilt in the squadron during active operations in fourteen weeks; eight machines were rebuilt in the same time. Wings and tail planes, rudders and tail skids, undercarriages and "props" too numerous to mention, came back on machines from offensive patrol shot through by Archy or riddled by machine gun bullets. They were quickly changed and the bus made serviceable for war flying.

In only one case was there any real delay—the famous case of the "R.A.F. wires, cross-bracing, centre section, upper," which on all the machines on our strength was shorter than the "Mob." tables showed or any the Park or Depot possessed. We measured and remeasured them. They were twenty-seven and a half inches from thread to thread. The Wing was incredulous. "If they are twenty-seven and a half inches, we will get them for you, but you had better be sure that all your

wires are twenty-seven and a half inches long or there will be trouble."
That was the Wing's last word. Once again C.O. and adjutant climbed
over the bus and again they measured the infernal wires.

"Twenty-seven and a half," shouted the C.O., delighted to have
something on the Wing. If the whole truth must be told, we had only
made the interesting discovery which gave rise to all this excitement
when Williams came back one day from patrol, having had a scrap
with five Fokkers, with his "cross-bracing wires, centre section, upper," cut away by Hun bullets that must have passed within an inch
of his head.

Who till then had ever thought of measuring a centre section
cross-bracing wire? The flat snipped wire was made into a scimitar-
shaped paper knife for Williams as a souvenir. We crossed the lines
on offensive patrol for the first time on July 15, 1918. The Front was
very quiet. It was Williams who brought down our first enemy aeroplane not far from Ostend,[1] with the famous Bassin de Chasse for
background, on July 20th, at about 9:45 in the morning. Early in the
afternoon the following message came from the Wing:

Signal Message
From: American Mission with Belgian Army.
To: CO. 17th Aero Squadron.
Re: confirmation E. A. sent down by Lieutenant Williams. 2nd
Section, 6 D. A., Belgian Army, reports one E.A. seen to go
down in flames S.W. of Ostend, between 9:30 and 10:00 this
morning.

On the same evening congratulatory telegrams on Williams' exploit came from General Salmond, commanding the R.A.F. in the
field, and from Colonel Cunningham. It was a great day with us
and the enlisted men were quite as excited as the officers. It meant
much that at last, after so many discouragements and changes, we had
achieved the beginning of our offensive career. Williams was given an
impromptu fete at dinner in the Mess which his retiring disposition
took with obvious embarrassment. Sergeant Kellum drew a large ink
sketch of the memorable "scrap" from the descriptions brought in by
the pilots. Ultimately it was framed and hung in the Mess with the
legend: "Our First Hun."

This too was the day on which we had our first casualty—Lieut.
George P. Glenn, a son of Virginia, and a charming fellow. He was

1. See Combat Report, No. 1.

missing from the morning patrol and was last seen diving steeply south of Ostend, after having been attacked by a Fokker at 20,000 feet.

We had many other memorable days at Petite Synthe. There was the day when Lieut. Floyd M. Showalter came down with engine trouble beyond the railway embankment, just south of Nieuport, in the floods of No Man's Land. Tipton flew low over him to protect him from being shot down by enemy scouts from above and, as he circled about him, he saw "Showie" calmly climb out of his bus and splash away west, wading toward the Belgian lines. Showalter told us later that he had found an underwater road, and after that we never ceased to "kid" him about his habit of wearing rubber boots when flying.

While we were escorting 211 Squadron, R.A.F., on the way home "Goodie," as Lieutenant Goodnow was known among us, in "B," for example, would take great delight in sitting right over "B" of the bombing formation, Gracie in "M" over "M," and 'A" over "A," and so on. "

Taking care of their big brothers" they called it, and it delighted No. 211 too. One of our most treasured letters is the following from Major G. R. M. Reid, M.C., of that squadron:

30th August, 1 918.

To Officer Commanding No. 65 Wing, Royal Air Force.

17th U. S. Aero Squadron:

I would very much like to express in writing the gratitude felt both by myself and the flying personnel under my command for the exceptionally fine escort work done by the above Squadron when escorting the bomb raids on Bruges Docks, carried out by this Squadron.

We are all agreed that when No. 17 Squadron was escorting our raid we had nothing to fear from A.E. Although it was often imperative to fly out to sea and attack from East of the Target, thus making it a very long trip over the lines, nevertheless No. 17 U. S. Squadron always stuck to us. On one or two occasions a machine of ours would straggle owing to engine trouble, but these machines had no need to fear attacking E.A. as some of the escorting machines would always look after the straggler.

On many occasions E.A. attempted to attack our bombing machines over the Target but they were never successful owing to the excellence of the escort.

TAKING CARE OF THEIR BIG BROTHERS

Finally I can only say that I do not consider that any Squadron in France could have supplied a better escort than No. 17 U. S. Aero Squadron.

(Sgd.) G. R. M. Reid,

Major R.A.F.

Commanding No. 211 Squadron.

This, as it were, supplemented a letter from the British Naval Authorities that reads as follows :

19th August, 1918.

To General Officer Commanding, Royal Air Force, B.E.F.
I should be glad if you would convey to Lieut.-Colonel Cunningham, D.F.C., the officers and men of the 65th Wing, R.A.F., an expression of my appreciation of the very good work done by them during the last month whilst cooperating with the 5th Group.
No. 211 Squadron has been particularly successful in their daylight attacks on *Bruges Docks* and *Shipping*, and 17th American Squadron also cooperated in the low bombing attack on *Varssenaere* aerodrome; in addition they have destroyed a lot of enemy machines.

(Sgd.) A. Boyle,

C. O. S.

for Vice-Admiral.

Major Reid's letter gave us unusual pleasure because the pilots of 211 Squadron, had been escorted during their career by Bristols and various kinds of scouts, and were famous for the criticism and "grousing" they had always levelled at the squadrons sent over to cover their bombing operations. It is an interesting fact too that, during the period in which we escorted them, not a machine of theirs was lost as a result of attack by enemy aircraft.

For months we had been without a medical officer, when suddenly by some mysterious vagary of the administration three doctors, each with a force of medical orderlies complete, descended upon us. It was an embarrassment of riches. How choose between them? One was an elderly gentleman from the South who wore gold-rimmed *pince-nez* and was painfully and feverishly concerned with the *minutiae* of the orders that had sent him trotting back and forth over the face of France. He was a captain and outranked our C. O., so it was obviously inappropriate for him to stay. Lieut. Jacob J. Ross, M. C, or R. M. C. as he was then and would have preferred to remain, was assigned in his stead, while the third and last of the sons of Æsculapius to arrive was transferred to other unknown fields of activity.

The choice was our great good fortune. Doctor Ross had seen much of college athletics from the inside. He had long experience and his enthusiasm for his job was vivifying. The sanitation of the camp was improved at once, although to do so was not an easy matter. He left no stone unturned to acquaint himself with the medical and surgical side of service in the field, but very especially he studied the ailments, diseases, and physical condition of flying officers. In this work the British gave him every opportunity for study and he was quick to realize how large a part temperament plays in a pilot's fitness for war work. He had a keen sense of the innate difference between a pilot who really didn't want to do his job, who was not of the stuff of which fighters are made, and the pilot who, however courageous, had been nervously shaken by the tension of flying and fighting over the lines.

"Old Doc," as he was affectionately called, had moreover a hobby that venereal disease could and must be stamped out, as a menace not only to the men themselves but to the success of our cause. This delicate subject he approached from so human an angle that the effect of his presence and counsel became forthwith apparent. He was big and strong and in his face one read a great sincerity. His interest was universal. He managed the flying officers as you would a football team in training, and the enlisted men as you would the students of a technical school. In his free time on days of bad weather he tried to see as much as he could of service at the front, visiting all nearby hospitals and clearing stations, helping the British with "sick call" and medical attention in neighbouring squadrons, or assisting at operations through the night when the wounded were pouring into the C.C.S. near Doullens, during the first days of the British push. In his unabated zeal for informing experience he was so often in quest of transportation on rainy days that he became known as the first of the "tender-hounds."

We celebrated the Glorious Fourth with a baseball game between the 148th Aero Squadron and ourselves. The French doctors and officers of *Train Sanitaire 2bis*, as well as our English friends, were invited. During the struggle a foul-fly caught on the head and bowled over Major Robert Lorraine, who was at that time in command of 211 Squadron, R.A.F., and was watching the game from the "bleachers." He bobbed up again smiling, never having lost his monocle—a feat that apparently drew this comment from an old French artillery officer, very smart in bright baggy trousers and scarlet *kepi*, who had been eyeing the play quizzically through drooping glasses: "*Mais, c'est très interessant! Ça. ressemble beaucoup à tennis, n'est-ce pas?*"

The Squadron Office was not really organized in a thorough-going way until we reassembled at Petite Synthe. It had then to carry on the voluminous paper work of a British fighting squadron, as well as the paper work required of a unit in the American armies. We were attached for the latter to the Second Corps, which had its Statistical Office at Fruges. Sgt. Hayden C Kellum, and Cpls. Lamonte P. Koop and William H. Reed, did devoted work in this branch of our activity and helped much to make records and operations go smoothly.

The weather was warm and hazy on August first, the wind light and falling. The first patrol of nine machines left at eight in the morning and went down the lines east of La Bassée. There they encountered, at nine o'clock, three Fokker triplanes and a Fokker biplane. The latter Lieut. Robert M. Todd attacked at between 14,000 and 16,000 feet and sent it crashing into a little wood near Provin.[2]

Thirty minutes later they came upon three Fokker biplanes and one Pfalz scout, between Wytschaete and Hollebeke, at 15,000 feet. Ten encounters took place and Lieut. William H. Shearman drove the Pfalz out of control, while Lieuts. M. K. Spidle and Ralph D. Gracie each drove down a Fokker biplane.[3]

In this fierce and wild dog-fight we never lost the upper hand for a single instant and, when the patrol returned and the pilots crowded, all excitement, into the adjutant's office, filling its warm sunniness with the icy chill of the upper air that still clung to their flying clothes, one was put to it, for a moment, to disentangle the tactics of the battle or its results from their furious colloquies, one with another, in which emphatic gestures illustrated, with fantastic vividness, side-slips, rolls, zooms, stalls, dives, loops, vertical banks, and all the tension and determination and lightning-quick reactions of imminent danger defied and overcome.

Out of that patrol a great confidence was born. The news spread like wildfire through the camp and, although Todd alone could absolutely claim his Hun, we knew now that our future as a fighting unit was safe. The pilots went off happy to their quarters, full of eagerness and a sense of power, while a busy telephone transmitted the news to

---

2. See Combat Report, No. 2
3. See Combat Reports, Nos. 3, 4, and 5.

the Wing and rattling typewriters, working at top speed, wrote out the mosaic of significant and indispensable details in combat reports. With these the orderlies then flew about the camp, like newsboys rushing out some extra about an earthquake, looking for the pilots to get their signatures.

When it became apparent that we were to leave the 65th Wing, it was decided to give a dinner—a "proper" dinner—to the higher officers under whom we had served in the Royal Air Force. Many of the pilots who had flown with British squadrons invited their old C. O.'s. Letters of invitation were written and confided to Wilcavage, the dispatch rider, who took a prolonged trip of constant riding for two days to deliver them. Gen. E. R. Ludlow-Hewitt, D. S. O., M. C, 10th Brigade; Lieut. Col. J. A. Cunningham, D. F. C, C. O. 65th Wing; Major G. R. M. Reid, M. C, C. O. 211 Squadron; Major Bell, M. C, D. S. O., C. O. 210 Squadron; Major R. Collishaw, D. S. O., D. S. C, D. F. C; Major C. T. Maclaren, C. O. 206 Squadron; Major W. S. Douglas, M. C, C. O. 84 Squadron; Major G. R. Howard, D. S. O., CO. 18 Squadron; Lieut. Col. B. F. Moore, C. O. 1 A. S. D. were invited.

A French chef was found at Dunkirk, a menu prepared after much debate, wines bought and flags of the Allies, and the whole camp licked into top-notch shape. It was a great evening and on the morning following—a clear fine morning—we "put on" what was, in many ways, one of the most spectacular and successful enterprises in which the squadron took part—the Varssenaere Aerodrome "show."

The field in question, which was situated southwest of Bruges, was of great extent and housed not less than five squadrons of Gothas and Fokkers. Plans for attacking it in great force and by surprise were carefully laid and contemplated originally the co-operation of four Camel squadrons—a number which was cut down to three, when the 148th moved out of the 65th Wing. The raid was finally confided to and carried out by 210 and 213 Squadrons, R. A. F., and the 17th Aero Squadron. The rendezvous was to be over the sea, and the machines, after they had assembled, were to fly inland and attack the aerodrome at dawn and in the order given above. Each machine was to carry four 20-lb. Cooper bombs, with the exception of the flight commanders' which were to carry phosphorus bombs to be dropped on or near the machine gun emplacements that guarded the aerodrome.

A practice flight over the British aerodrome at Andembert, near Calais, was made some days before the date set for the real attack, and on that occasion a phosphorus bomb was exploded in the air over

*Our attack on Varssenaere Aerodrome, August 13, 1918*

Fort Mardick, between Dunkirk and Gravelines, to mark the rallying point. It looked like a huge dense white mushroom hung in the clear blue sky, until it gradually dissipated over the sea. From there the squadrons proceeded to and dived on Andembert aerodrome, climbing away one after the other in strictest predetermined formation to avoid collisions. Colonel Cunningham, Major Fowler, and our C. O. "sat overhead" in their Camels to superintend and criticise this preliminary flight.

After several postponements due to bad weather, it was finally decided to attack on August 13th. Before it was light the 17th left our field in formation and disappeared in the pre-dawn mist. Soon afterwards those who had watched them go saw a light fired over the sea and knew that the rendezvous was made. Two hours of anxious waiting followed, for this was the most dangerous job we had yet undertaken. The Royal Air Force *Communiqué* describes the attack as follows:

A raid was carried out by No. 17 American Squadron on Varssenaere Aerodrome, in conjunction with Squadrons of the 5th Group. After the first two Squadrons had dropped their bombs from a low height, machines of No. 17 American Squadron dived to within 200 feet of the ground and released their bombs, then proceeded to shoot at hangars and huts on the aerodrome, and a *château* on the N.E. corner of the aerodrome was also attacked with machine gun fire. The following damage was observed to be caused by this combined operation: a dump of petrol and oil was set on fire, which appeared to set fire to an ammunition dump; six Fokker biplanes were set on fire on the ground, and two destroyed by direct hits from bombs; one large Gotha hangar was set on fire and another half demolished; a living hut was set on fire and several hangars were seen to be smouldering as the result of phosphorus bombs having fallen on them. In spite of most of the machines taking part being hit at one time or another, all returned safely, favourable ground targets being attacked on the way home.

Colonel Cunningham, who had "gone over" with our squadron, was the first to return. He jumped out of his machine and said: "I got a Hun!" In the morning haze he had lost the formation but found an enemy two-seater out at sea and had shot it down near the beach.

Then one by one the pilots came back, their machines badly shot up, but they themselves safe and sound. Everything had worked as scheduled. The 210th and 213th had dropped their bombs and had climbed away and circled round as protection, while our pilots went down and finished the exploit by dropping bombs on the *château*, in which the Hun officers lived, the hangars, the men's quarters, and the workshops. They then flew round and round the aerodrome at from fifty to two hundred feet from the ground, diving on and shooting at machines lined up with engines "turning over" preparatory to "taking off," as well as at enemy mechanics and pilots scattered about the field. Of the machines on the ground our pilots were sure that they had "got" at least seven; the British hovering above confirmed the destruction of eight.

Months later a captured German revealed the fact that in all fourteen had been put out of action. One of 210 Squadron's pilots on his return reported having seen Todd chase a German flying officer out of his machine and around a hangar and that Todd then dodged around the other side of the hangar and cut him off. What damage was done to the German personnel could never be accurately determined, but reports came in from Belgium, when the Belgian and British armies reached the vicinity of Bruges, that over one hundred and twenty soldier mechanics and about thirty pilots had been killed.[4]

The destruction of Varssenaere aerodrome brought us immediate recognition from General Salmond and a little later a telegram of warm congratulation from the Chief of the American Air Service followed by this letter:

General Headquarters American Expeditionary Forces
Office of the Chief Air Service
August 23, 1918.

From: Chief Air Service, American E. F.
    To: Major H. Fowler, A.S.
Subject: Work of 17th Aero Squadron.

*1.* This office is in receipt of your letter of August 16th enclosing the details of the work of the 17th Aero Squadron on August 13th in its attack of the German airdrome at Varssenaere. Chief of Air Service is particularly pleased with the splendid work done by this squadron on the date mentioned. It shows the aggressiveness and working together as a squadron, which we are endeavouring to obtain for all units of the American Air

4. See report.

Service.

2. I have furnished a copy of your report to the Intelligence Section, General Staff, who have informed me that they were greatly pleased with the work done and have cabled the information back to the United States for publication.

3. Please express to the Squadron Commander, pilots and soldiers of the Squadron the appreciation of the Chief Air Service for the excellent work performed by them.

(Sgd.) R. O. Van Horn,

Colonel, A.S.,

Assistant, C.A.S.

For and in the absence of C.A.S.

The Germans had apparently found out by this time who we were and where we lived, and they paid us an indirect compliment—a compliment of feeble imitation—on the mastery of our attack. A week after the raid and, as it happened, two days after we had left Petite Synthe (evidently this move was unknown to them), the officers and men of 211 Squadron were awakened just at dawn by rapid repeated *rafales* of machine gun fire from the air. Some of them ran out and, behold a solitary Fokker diving and then zooming and diving again and again, firing from close to the ground burst after vindictive burst into our empty shacks and hangars.

But Varssenaere was not the only "high point," during the period in which we lived at Petite Synthe and patrolled the Belgian Front, from Zeebrugge to the northern end of the British lines in the region of Mount Kemmel and the Forest of Nieppe. The sector was one on which Hun scouts were wary, and yet we succeeded in shooting down nine of them, confirmed,[5] while with others we had many a scrap, far and high over enemy bases of supply, the results of which could never—unfortunately for the length of the string of our victories—be accurately known.

On the offensive patrol of August 12th, hangs an amusing tale. It was a day when some fighting of the fiercest kind took place "Over Ostend," after we had escorted 211's bombers to their perpetual target—the submarine shelters, marine works, and docks at Bruges. These encounters have not been recorded in "Combat Reports," but in the *mêlée* Lieut. William J. Armstrong, Lieut. Ralph W. Snoke, and Lieut. Harriss P. Alderman, or more familiarly "Aldy," were wounded.

---

5. See Combat Reports, Nos. 6, 7, 8, 9, 10, 11, 12, 13, 14, 15, and 16.

They were sent to Queen Alexandra Hospital, which stood not far from our aerodrome, near the little French fort from which Archy fired sometimes as many as six hundred rounds a night at the relays of Gothas that went overhead on their way to Dunkirk or Calais.

Armstrong's wound was rather serious. He had had just strength enough to get back to the field where he "sat down" all too violently, with the wind behind him, on the back of a standing D.H. 9. That did not improve his condition. Aldy's "missive" from the Hun had come through his petrol tank from which it went on, as he put it, to "where he sat." The flood of petrol that instantly covered him convinced him that he was mortally wounded, but he hung on gamely and succeeded in gliding west, making the beach a mile beyond Nieuport, on our side of things. We did not hear from him for some time, for the Belgians "captured" him as a suspicious character. Lieut. Robert M. Todd, when he climbed out of his machine, said he believed Aldy had gone down into the sea and he told the tale that way to Army.

Army felt a deep responsibility; he had been flight leader in this show and, when later Aldy was brought in from the operating room, just as Armstrong was coming out of the ether, the latter did not know whether both were alive or both dead. His mind was back in the scrap, and the consciousness of the sportsmanship they looked for from one another was strong upon him. Over his bed some flies hung in the air. He took them for Fokkers sailing about high, high up. The nurse tried to calm him: "They are only flies," she said. But he, unpersuaded, reached out his hand and clutched an imaginary stick while, working it around in front of him and throwing himself about on the bed, as in vertical banks, half rolls, and zooms, with his eyes glued on the flies, he drawled:

"Come on, Aldy! There they are, up there, the —— —— dogs. But they won't come down and fight; they won't come down! Stick with me, Aldy; we'll show them where we're from. We'll crash the last —— —— one of them."

So he manoeuvred and manoeuvred about on his bed vainly trying to get on the tail of one of those flies.

The next day, after much bustle and fuss of orderlies and nurses to get the hospital into fitting shape. His Majesty, King George, arrived to inspect it. Aldy and Army knew, as they lay there, something of the suspense that must precede being given a V.C., though they did not kid themselves with visions of such heights. The King came down their ward, very simply, with a word for every wounded man—an expression of interest, a touch of sympathy. When he reached Snoke, he said: "Ah, some Americans! I hope you are quite all right. I see you were wounded in the head."

And then to Army: "How are you, and where were you wounded?"

"In the back and arm, Your Majesty."

Finally he reached Aldy with: "Ah, another! And where were you wounded?"

Aldy had a terrible moment of self-consciousness, but his quick-witted reply was: "Over Ostend, Your Majesty."

The King understood. A smile of delighted amusement crept over his face and spread to the faces of the officers of his suite. Aldy's wound became, from that moment, as it were, a public possession, and its exact location was always thereafter described in polite society—for had not a king understood?—as "Over Ostend."

HAMILTON GETS A BALLOON

CHAPTER 3

# The Beginning of the British Drive
# for Cambrai

On August 18th we were ordered to move to Auxi-le-Château. Word came at 11 o'clock at night, while the Hun was overhead, and we were ready to pull out at dawn. We arrived the next day, covered with the deep white dust of the road from Dunkirk, through St. Omer, Fruges, and Hesdin. At the entrance of our new field. Brig. Gen. C. A. H. Longcroft, D.S.O., Col. P. H. L. Playfair, M.C., O.C. 3rd Brigade, R.A.F., and a number of other staff officers were waiting to welcome us—a courtesy we shall not soon forget.

At Auxi our aerodrome was delightfully situated. It lay on rising ground, to the southeast of the town, on the old Auxi-le-Château-Crécy Road. The officers' tents, well dug in, were peppered down a slope under the edge of a little forest of small trees where owls hooted at night and in which later the C.O. had his hut.

On the first patrol we sent over the lines (August 21st) from Auxi, Lieutenant Showalter drove down one enemy machine, and on the afternoon show. Lieutenants Tipton and Campbell each drove down one. Lieutenant Williams drove down two out of control, and Lieutenant Hamilton destroyed another.[1]

The push was now on that began at Château Thierry, and we were called upon to make a continuous and extraordinary effort in those momentous hours. Low bombing and machine gun attacks on balloons and infantry were the order of the day, and we sent out two machines at a time all day long, from dawn to dark.

On one of these bombing shows (August 23 rd)[2] there was an

1. See Combat Reports, Nos. 17, 18, 19, 20, 21, and 23.
2. See Bombing Report, No. 2.

incident—among many more or less dramatic of the same kind that it would require pages to chronicle—which was always known among us as "Williams' Show." The R.A.F. thought it worthy of being recorded as follows in their official *communiqué*:

Lieutenant Williams, 17th American Squadron, was shot in the back and his petrol tank pierced by machine gun fire. In spite of his wound he came back with his finger stopping the hole in the petrol tank and landed successfully after having engaged transport from a height of 100 feet.

During the next four days we shot down a balloon a day, with the exception of the 23rd when we put on low bombing shows exclusively.[3] It was on one of these expeditions that Lieutenant Hamilton, one of the most fearless and expert pilots we ever had, was shot down from the ground just as he was zooming away from the "sausage" he had set on fire—his second in two days.

It was the nature of the fighting on the ground, while the Hun was going back, that worked so complete a change in our operations. The Air Force of the enemy was largely concentrated in the vicinity of Cambrai, but the congestion on the roads behind his lines gave us an opportunity of doing greater damage to his morale and material by attacks on moving infantry and transport, than we could ever have accomplished by devoting all our attention to his scouts. The latter, for the most part, flew in very large flocks and, except for sallies from time to time against small detached flights of Allied machines, they waged a defensive offensive.

It was but natural, however, that they should make low-bombing and machine gun attacks on ground targets hazardous in the extreme. That was no doubt part of their business. In other words they were there, but we, when carrying out such machine gun attacks and especially when loaded with bombs and flying a height of a few hundred feet, had few chances to attack and "get" them.[4] We depended upon other squadrons patrolling higher up, at various levels, to look out for Fokkers, while we did a job that cost us casualties and doubtless too a certain quota of what would have been our legitimate toll of Huns during these furious days.

In many ways, on the other hand, "ground-straffing" is a severer test than most fighting of a pilot's stamina and skill and of the rigging and fitting of his machine. Perhaps too this work of ours helped more

---

3. See Combat Reports, Nos. 22, 24, and 28.
4. For other encounters of this period, see Combat Reports, Nos. 25, 26, 27, and 29.

to bring the end of the war a little nearer than if we had shot down many enemy scouts in that first week. From Intelligence we knew that our attacks did much to shatter the German soldier's faith in his own airmen. At all events we came down on the Hun without cessation, as he retired in the direction of Cambrai, shooting up his convoys that became a wild confusion of broken lorries and runaway horses, and scattering his infantry from the roads into the fields, inflicting on them many casualties.[5] From the ground over which our pilots buzzed the Hun sent up all manner of "stuff" from Archy to pom-poms and a hail of machine gun fire. But no feat was too daring for them, and their extremely manoeuvrable machines made their work only the more spectacular.

It was on one of these raids that George Wise disappeared. His engine failed and he was made prisoner. Merton Campbell too was "missing" on the 23rd, and when the Boche had gone back beyond Thiepval and Contalmaison we found his grave. He had landed, up-side down, in that broad belt of shell-torn country where there is not a yard not shattered by heavy explosive. His grave was a low soft mound beside his crashed machine. On it the usual inverted bottle, stuck in the mud, contained an envelope, blood-soaked and bearing his name.

We made a cross of a broken four-bladed "prop" of fine mahogany that we got from salvage, and engraved a nameplate on a copper disk. We took it up past wrecked villages and then more wrecked villages, into the old No Man's Land of some of the fiercest battles of the war. At the head of his grave without ceremony we set it up. He lies there, one of our stoutest, by a file of tree trunks smashed and stripped and grotesquely rigid against the sun, under a little slope of ground rising toward the east that has been blasted into dust by months of artillery fire.

Both Hamilton and Campbell were at once awarded the Distin-guished Flying Cross by the British and their people notified.

The twenty-sixth of August was our most tragic day. It had rained in the night and a gusty wind had begun to blow at dawn, getting stronger and gustier as the day advanced. Low clouds, with gaps of blue between them, streamed thickly up from the southwest over the rolling hills beyond the aerodrome. Our Besseneaux hangars bulged up and flapped; our tents were all swollen on one side and lean and caved in, against the wind, on the other; the aeroplane fabric that cov-

5. See Bombing Reports, Nos. 1, 2, 3, 4, 5, 6, 7, 8, and 9.

ered the holes we called our windows, in the Squadron Office shack, were bellied and tense; the little wood was full of the noise of the wind. It was blowing in fits at seventy or eighty miles an hour.

At four thirty in the afternoon the colonel rang up and said that there were a lot of Huns about on the lines and that some of our "low-straffers" were in trouble on the Bapaume-Cambrai Road.

Tipton, who was called upon to lead the patrol, had been moody and silent ever since Hamilton had "gone West" (August 24th). He sat in the Mess all day long and played the gramophone to himself, holding his big, slightly bald, blond head in his hands, a dead cigar in the corner of his mouth. He was "fed-up." He did nothing but stare into the gramophone, while it wheezed and growled and squeaked out "*Old Bill Bailey,*" "*The Mississippi Volunteers,*" or "*Poor Butterfly.*"

"Tip" got the patrol away in good style and they disappeared— eleven of them—over the trees. One machine returned before long with engine trouble, then another with guns jammed. Two hours passed. Then Goodie and Snoke arrived. Some of us will never forget the look in Goodie's light blue eyes, as he stood in the dusk, with his back against the door between the Squadron Office and the Pilots' Room. There was a huge map of the Third British Army front on the wall behind him. He pointed out where "it" happened, and slowly, bit by bit, from him and Snoke we got the story[6] while he continued to stare, seeing us only a little, at the fight that was stamped almost visible on his eyes. He and "Snokie" seemed horrified and crest-fallen—all broken up—to be standing there, though each of them had put up a wonderful show, when Tip and Todd and Frost and Jackson and Bittinger and Roberts had not returned. Dixon too was missing; but after a long wait, in which we gave him up as lost, he came "hedge-hopping" over the trees, having been driven down almost to the ground and having lost his way in the driving mist and high wind.

What really happened was this. Their mission, as we have said, was to cover low bombing operations, as it turned out, of the 148th Aero Squadron. On crossing the lines five Fokkers were noticed climbing east of Quéant at about five o'clock. Immediately afterward the five Fokkers in question were seen to attack a Camel at a height of about 1,000 feet. The patrol at once went down to the assistance of the Camel (afterward identified as that of Lieut. George Seibold of the 148th Squadron) and attacked the enemy machines. Several other flights of Fokkers were then observed coming down through rifts

6. See Combat Reports, Nos. 30, 31, 32, and 33.

48

in the clouds from 6,000 feet. The wind was blowing furiously into Hunland. A general engagement took place in which still other flights of Fokkers came down from higher up.

In addition to the Combat Reports referred to, Lieutenant Dixon fired indecisively at a number of other enemy machines, as did Lieutenants Goodnow and Snoke. The latter's Camel was riddled with machine-gun fire and he only just succeeded in getting back to the aerodrome, pursued over the lines by a number of Fokkers sitting on his tail and firing without let-up.

That was our worst day. Jackson had got his permission to cross the lines only a day or two before, and Roberts had returned from hospital within the preceding twenty-four hours. We gave them all up for lost, but more than a month later a postcard came through the Aviation Officer in London from Tipton. He seemed chiefly concerned to know what had become of the much-prized Hun rifle that he had found on one of his expeditions to the front lines. He remarked however, *en passant*, that in going down he had got two Huns and that Todd, before he landed, had added another to his string. He, Todd, and Frost were prisoners. Bittinger has also been reported a prisoner from other sources, but the exact circumstances of his fate still remain obscure.

The Mess had an undercurrent that night that it seldom had. But on the surface we still carried on without any false pride in our stiff upper lip. It was a hard blow—two flight commanders and eight pilots within a week. We consoled ourselves with the thought that they had done more damage than we had received. That was something, and that was the spirit with which we and the British fought.

For about a week the British wisely kept us out of the fray. New busses arrived. New pilots were assigned, notably Lieut. George A. Vaughn who had been doing fine work with 84 Squadron, R.A.F. He was placed in command of "B" flight. Lieut. William T. Clements came from the 148th Aero Squadron as flight commander of "C" flight.

What we felt, in the weeks that followed, to be our chief reason for pride—and to some of us it was a matter of astonishment—was that in spite of the naturally sobering effect of such a day, we could have defied the most critical eye to discern any abatement in the impetuosity of our flights' attacks, any relaxation in their unfaltering audacity and devotion to their duty of "doing in" the Hun or, day by day, helping in large and larger measure to chase him from the skies. We carried the battle far over the enemy lines. We did not penetrate now as far, of course, as we had on certain patrols from Dunkirk when we operated more than thirty miles over in hostile territory. This latter feat—in itself no mean achievement for scout machines equipped with rotary motors—could not be repeated on the front of the greatest battles of the war where the enemy had thrown in prodigally his best and largest "circuses." In other words, in the face of any losses we sustained, the pilots kept intact or, in some cases, increased the intensity of their offensive spirit.

Life went on at Auxi. On "dud" days we sent to Abbeville and Boulogne for little luxuries for the Mess. We improvised a band out of old shell-cases on which Vaughn used to beat out hurrying rhythms of "Coon Songs" and "Turkey Trots." We sent Aldy—he of the soft southern drawl and sometimes amusingly pointed speech—to buy a piano. He was gone all a long day of rain and mud, and came back after nightfall with a strange instrument of carved mahogany bearing conspicuously the date: 1856. At dinner he was very much kidded about his exploit, since he had been assured by his Frenchman that the carved mahogany box was perfectly in tune, its action perfect, and that it was a bargain at four hundred *francs*—this although every other key stayed "put" when struck and even the "*Mississippi Volunteers*" died away on it, after the first ten bars, into fragmentary notes that just survived amid the tumultuous rattle of shell-case and bottle traps, the blare of Schneider on a cornet, and the moan of a saxophone as the C.O. played it extemporaneously.

But all things are possible in an aero squadron. The piano—the great virtue of which Aldy afterward claimed was its portability, feeling perhaps that if he had not been a good mark for the Hun as he threw his bus around in the sky, he had been "touched" by one Frenchman, whom he had made rich beyond all expectation with his shower of American gold—the piano, *our* piano, was overhauled and made serviceable. Later we matched 87 Squadron, R.A.F., "doubles or nothing" for it and recovered two hundred *francs*.

While we were operating from the Auxi aerodrome, often in conjunction with the 148th Squadron, the line moved east rapidly and it was necessary for us to establish at Beugnâtre, near Bapaume, an advanced landing ground from which we took up wireless interception and devoted ourselves to attacking enemy two-seaters. A detail of mechanics, accompanied by a medical orderly, was sent forward and hangars erected. This site was that of an old British aerodrome, afterwards in the possession of the Hun. The trees were smashed,

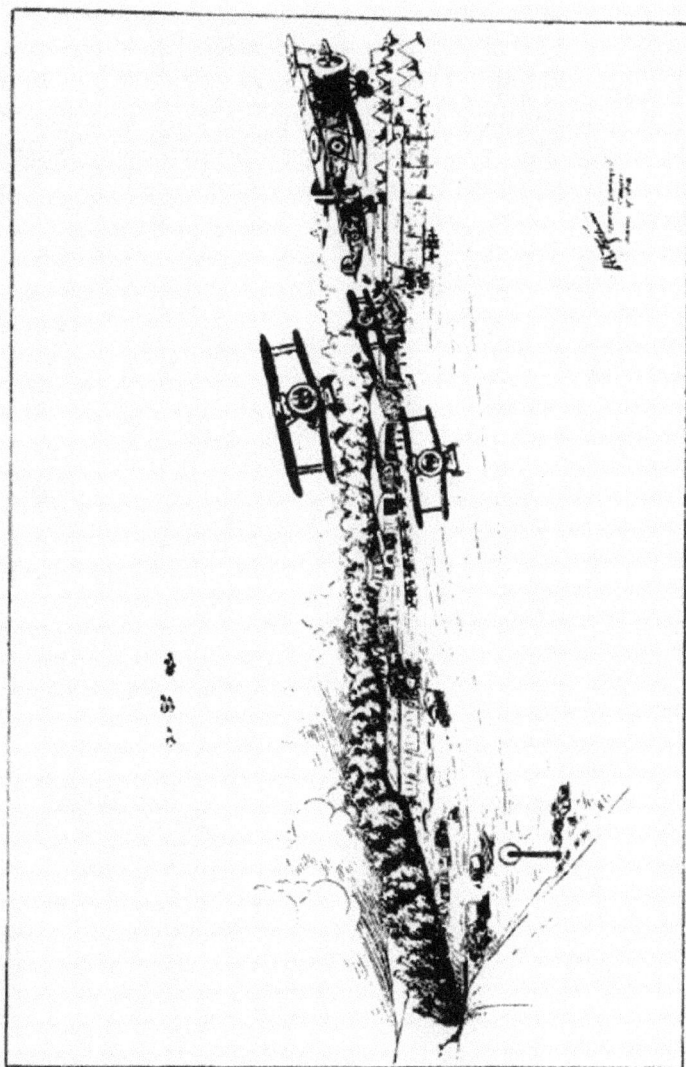

*Taking off in formation Aux-i-le-Château*

the numerous rusty Nissen huts that lined the road riddled and torn and caved in, the aerodrome a mass of shell holes (among which the R.E.8's, that shared it with us, landed on their first day out there), the quarters an unrecognizable heap of splinters, the road almost impassable. The Hun had constructed deep dugouts and, out of scraps of old sheet iron he had left about, quarters were erected and in them wireless apparatus established. The shell holes too were filled in. We kept a flight of machines there, from dawn to dusk, from September 10th to September 20th. The men and officers who went up to Beugnâtre on special duty came back to camp with a most marvellous collection of souvenirs.[7]

---

7. For other engagements of this period, see Combat Reports, Nos. 34, 35, 36, and 37.

*That musical mess at Sambrin*

CHAPTER 4

# The British Break the Cambrai Front

On September 20th we were ordered to proceed to Soncamp aerodrome, near Doullens, which was being vacated by No. 12 Corps Squadron, R.A.F., of R.E.8's. Eighty-seven Squadron, R.A.F., a Dolphin unit commanded by Major C. J. W. Darwin, D.S.O., was moving to the same field on the same day. It was cold and rainy and the clouds low and broken. The machines got away and the transport; stores and barrack bags, shops and officers' kits were packed, the camp at Auxi policed and we started.

Soncamp aerodrome is not far from the little town of Sombrin that lies rather scattered and nondescript—a typical French farming village—on the road through Grand Rullecourt to Frévent. It occupies—the aerodrome—the north side of a farm the house of which, enclosed in a large gray stone wall, suggests some relic of a small convent—an impression that the high archway into the great square farmyard strengthens. The hangars were permanent and of camouflaged corrugated iron. There were good Adrian huts as barracks for the enlisted men, and we pitched our officers' tents and the two marquees that were to be the Mess in a triangle of pasture, beside a growth of underbrush, at the upper end of the camp. To this end we also moved the old wooden shack that we made into a very comfortable Squadron Office, C.O.'s office, and pilots' room. Soon it was full of document files, maps, clicking typewriters, and miniature Hun aeroplanes.

The mud in this camp was omnipresent and deep. We waded through it constantly, for the hangars were divided between 87 Squadron and ourselves, and our Supply Office, men's mess, men's quar-

54

ters, and recreation hut, as well as our transport, armoury, petrol and ammunition dumps, were at the entrance of the aerodrome, entirely separated from the Squadron Office. On the day we moved in, the little by-road behind the hangars was blocked by a couple of lorries sunk deep in the mud that only unloading and many efforts succeeded in dislodging.

At Soncamp it poured off and on much of the time, and we slept in the damp and lived in the damp until a bright idea came to us. Ellison, who was resting after having "crashed" just inside of our lines with all controls shot away and three Fokkers on his tail peppering him everywhere but in the vital spot, carried it out with the help of others who turned to with the zest of men chilled to the bone. They built a fireplace, out of old red petrol tins filled with mud, in the side flap of one of the marquees. The smoke of the fire made its way chiefly, not up the elaborately calculated chimney of superimposed oil drums with their heads knocked out, but into the marquee itself where coughing, tearful forms moved about as in a mist. Yet that too was cured and the "Band" beat out "'N Everything" with new ardour, while "Smoke 'em out" and "Rummy" held sway on nights of drenching rain.

The trials and tribulations of the Mess Officer, Lieutenant Ayers, grew apace at Sombrin, for we were far from base supply depots which were, in fact, fast shutting up shop to follow the great advance of General Byng's army, and far too from the depots of the front that constantly moved away after the retreating Hun. "Grousing" made itself heard. Finally to help out. Lieutenant Giesecke, commonly known as "Gesooks," stepped into the breach. Among other innovations for our comfort, he contrived a toaster made of wire net and an unserviceable blowpipe, and was thereafter called "O. C. Toast."

We opened the Soncamp chapter with a flourish on September 22nd. While on the morning patrol. Lieutenant Vaughn saw fifteen Fokkers dive, as he thought, on our "C" flight formation from 15,000 feet. Though outnumbered nearly five to one, he led his flight impetuously to the attack and, in the midst of furious and numerous "bursts" fired by all our pilots, the results of which could not be observed because of the bewildering intensity of the engagement, he shot down one Fokker in flames and crashed another, while Lieutenants Wicks and Knotts accounted for two more. In all over thirty enemy machines were engaged on this patrol alone.[1]

Lieut. Theose E. Tillinghast, whose health at the time was so frail

1. See Combat Reports, Nos. 38, 39, 40, 41, and 42.

that he was constantly dodging the doctor and whose veins were blue under the thin skin of his temples, yet who would never give up flying and fighting, was missing from this scrap. He afterward turned up in London, with a most amusing tale to tell of how he escaped through a hole in the roof of the house "they" had locked him up in, made his way from Valenciennes to Belgium, where he got a suit of civilian clothes, and was passed from Belgian home to Belgian home at night, as it were by schedule, on a regular underground railway. Finally he reached Brussels where he moved about the streets freely, greatly enjoying himself and his precarious situation.

He even went to the length, it seems, of taking a trolley ride to a neighbouring German aerodrome which he inspected carefully and at length. There, or in Brussels, he became fast friends with a most opportune person—the Belgian engineer who ran the electric plant from which the current for charging the frontier wire barrier was drawn. The latter amiably let him into all his official secrets with regard to which wires were charged and which not, supplied him with rubber gloves and a pair of nippers and, having set the hour for his crossing over, gave him final formal instructions about making good his escape. This "Tilly," as we called Tillinghast, did to his own immense satisfaction.

From this patrol Lieut. Gerald P. Thomas also failed to return. We missed from the Mess, more than we admitted to ourselves, "Tommy's" quiet manner, his boyish clean simplicity, his steady blue eyes and bright blond hair. Often, very often, one heard his name spoken. He had never thrust himself forward, but had done his job unostentatiously and simply. Almost without our realizing it he had made a deep dent in our memory.

September 22nd is, in yet another sense, one of our days. The order conferring on Vaughn the Distinguished Flying Cross, for which on that very 22nd he had again so valorously shown his especial worthiness, bears, as it were by a strange coincidence, that date. Here is the order:

Routine Orders
by
General F. M. H. S. Rawlinson, Bart.,
G.O.V.O., K.C.B., K.C.M.G.
Commanding Fourth Army

September 22, 1918.

Military Secretary's Branch

2533 (a). Immediate Rewards (a). Under authority delegated by His Majesty the King, the Field Marshal Commanding-in-Chief has made the following awards for gallantry and devotion to duty in action:

The Distinguished Flying Cross.

Lieutenant G. A. Vaughn, United States Air Force, attached Royal Air Force

H. C. Holman, Major-General,
D.A. and Q.M.G., Fourth Army.

Later, and for no less reason, Burdick and Knotts were similarly decorated by the British.

Dud weather now set in with a vengeance. But the offensive went on. The line changed from day to day. Those were the days of the great battles, on the Third Army Front, for the Canal du Nord, the Hindenburg Line, the Canal de l'Escaut, and Cambrai. As the Boche retreated, even through cloud and rain, we bombed his transport and troop concentrations in the sunken roads near Esnes and Estourmel. Of Awoingt station, or "Up Wink" as the pilots called it, we made a special target and touched off its munition dumps.[2]

Two days after our arrival at our new station Lieutenant Knotts took a new pilot, Lieut. Edgar G. White, out to show him the lines and, having waggled to him to "go home," went over and dived on a German convoy that he saw moving from Cambrai toward Bapaume. As he fired, he turned his "tracers" along the roadside into an ammunition dump, that immediately blew up. The explosion was formidable and was reported, independently, as a feature of the day at the Front, by Lieutenant Springs of the 148th Aero Squadron and by a ground officer of 59 Squadron, R.A.F., who was stationed at the Advanced Landing Ground. Both observed from far off the immense column of smoke that it made and, at the moment, without knowledge of the cause.[3]

Knotts too it was who a little later "pulled" the famous stunt of pursuing a closed Hun staff car through the village of Naves and down a road, from about fifty feet from the ground, until it overturned in the ditch. "Its occupants fell out," he remarked laconically, on reporting to the Squadron Office, "and one of them got up and ran. I fired at him. The other did not move."

---

2. See Bombing Reports, Nos. 14, 15, 17, 18, 19, 20, 24, 25, 27, and 30.

3. See Bombing Report, No. 10.

Over and over again, as the battle for Cambrai progressed, our patrols met and made sallies at a large formation of blue-tailed Fokkers. We tried to ambush them in the clouds or, on clear days, we sailed around in an unconcerned and unguarded kind of a way, hoping to coax them nearer to our lines. The "Blue-Tails" did much the same to us. They were a stout "bunch" that needed really no coaxing at all, if for a moment they "had it on us" even a little in numbers, and several times we got into some fairly good "close-ups" with them. As flyers they were by far the best Huns and, as fighters, the most aggressive, we had ever encountered. The Blue-Tails were in fact, as we found out afterwards, one of the most famous of the Boche organizations and well known for their depredations on other fronts.

For a couple of days we "curtsied" to them, passing the time of day at long range, and we knew perfectly well that, sooner or later, something was bound to happen, especially as, at that time, we were making a business of "picking on" enemy two-seaters. On September 24th, at 10 o'clock in the morning, our formation of fourteen machines saw, rather far off, an enemy formation of thirteen, accompanied by two other formations of eight each. Nothing happened. Fifteen minutes later one of our flights dived to 5,000 feet on two two-seaters and chased them scuttling past the canal south of Cambrai. They were bait, for not long afterward, as our flights were buzzing along, at about 9,000 feet over Havrincourt Woods, a formation of sixteen Blue-Tails dropped on them without warning from 16,000 or 17,000 feet, while a number of other Fokkers "sat upstairs" waiting for their best moment to pounce on us.

Fokkers dive well; they had the "jump" on us at last; and our luck for the moment was bad: four of our machines were incapacitated on the spot with gun-jams and C. C. gears out of action. But the other ten took up the gage thrown down, and before the spluttering *rat-tat-tat-tat* of machine guns on all sides had ceased we had taken a toll of five destroyed and one driven down out of control, without losing a single pilot or machine.[4] Later, on the same day, the 148th "hopped" the Blue-Tails, or what remained of them, and cleaned up six of them.

This picturesquely painted enemy circus was never again seen on the Front.

We did even better on September 28th. It was a very lively day

---

4. See Combat Reports, Nos. 43, 44, 45, 46, 47, 48, 49, 50, and 5. For September 27th, see Combat Report, No. 52.

Running down a German Staff car

just "east of Cambrai." Low bombing attacks on Up Wink (Awoingt), where enemy troops were reported heavily concentrated, were only part of the entertainment.[5] On the evening patrol, Lieut. Howard Burdick shot down two Fokkers and Lieutenant Vaughn one, in a general dogfight, in which there were not a few indecisive, or if decisive unrecorded, furious close-range encounters.[6] In the midst of the general mix-up, while the rest of the flight were sharply engaged, four Fokkers got on Lieutenant Wicks' tail and working together drove him literally to the ground. Wicks never lost his head. He dodged and ducked, half rolled, zigzagged and gamely fought on, turning again and again on his pursuers, until he was down so near "the carpet" that, after the last dive he made before shaking them off, he stove in the leading edge of his wings on the branches of trees, as he zoomed past a Fokker out of a little clearing just inside which the scrap finally ended.

During the latter part of September and the greater part of October, as our bombing reports show,[7] we brought discomfiture to the Hun in many forms and helped to break up the organization of his retreat toward the frontier, in spite of continued unfavourable weather of low-hanging mists and drizzling rain. We added much valuable material to British Intelligence, which made it possible to strike the enemy ceaselessly and at his weakest spot. We took an active part in those well-regulated and hammering blows, fighting hostile infantry and machine gun nests more than we fought Hun scouts and observation planes.

But we did not fail, on the other hand, to take advantage of whatever opportunity his waning forces in the air gave us. Vaughn and Burdick especially never considered a bombing show complete unless they hunted out and attacked one of the German two-seaters which were vainly attempting to regulate the fire of Boche batteries or watch British movements on the ground. Together they accounted for a D.F.W. and a Halberstadt, in addition to the L.V.G. biplane that Vaughn shot down alone toward the end of September.[8]

Soon the line began to approach Le Cateau and we were ordered to hold ourselves in readiness to move.[9] Estourmel was selected as an

---

5. See Bombing Report, No. 14.
6. See Combat Reports, Nos. 53, 54, and 55.
7. See Bombing Reports, Nos.11 to 33 inclusive.
8. See Combat Reports, Nos. 54, 56, and 57.
9. For our last victories, see Combat Reports, Nos. 58 and 59.

advanced landing ground, and Esnes as the site of a new aerodrome from which we were to operate. The "staff" went up in cars to look over the lay of the land and make preparations. In going one passed through the whole depth of the battlefields of four years, from Saulty dump, near Doullens, that the Huns had shelled during their great offensive of March and April, through villages at first touched only here and there by shell fire, on to villages torn and smashed, with gaping roofs and caving walls, to villages in the midst of the old battlefield, where nothing lived but weeds and where only a sign, mud-covered, in the midst of the brick dust and abandoned German material, remained to tell that a village once was there.

This waste is wide on the Cambrai front. Finally new battlefields were crossed—caked clay fresh in shell craters, extemporized bridges, and villages more or less "done in"—and Cambrai reached with its blackened square and torn railway tracks. From there we moved across a green country full of dead Huns lying in the tawny grass with their guns and tanks, rifles, machine guns, mess tins, broken transport, and piled shells and stores.

This was the region on which our pilots had looked down while they watched for enemy movements on the ground or Fokkers in the air. It seemed in some way to belong to us, although in it now all the fever of war was dead.

But we did not move into that region to take part in the battles which were fast approaching the scene of the earliest engagements between the Germans and the First Hundred Thousand—Mons and Maubeuge. We were to "go South," which to us meant going to our own armies. We heard the news with mixed emotions. We wanted naturally to have some part in the exploits of our own people in the field. But we had been very happy with the British and had learned their game and how well they played it.

The order came to turn in our British supplies, which was done, and we prepared to entrain. The day before our departure (October 31st) General Longcroft flew over in his Camel and asked that he might say a few words to all ranks. The enlisted men were drawn up on three sides of a hangar and he walked down their lines asking, here and there, one or another of them what his work had been before the war and in the Squadron. He then read to officers and men the following letter from General Byng, commander of the Third British Army.

Headquarters,
Third Army, B.E.F.
30th October, 1918.

Dear Longcroft:

Will you please convey to the Commanders and all ranks of the 17th and 148th American Squadrons my sincere appreciation of their excellent and valuable work with the Third Army, and thank them very warmly for so cordially responding to all the calls made upon them. I greatly regret their departure and wish them every luck.

Sincerely,

(Sgd.) J. Byng. 52

He added simply and briefly, but very feelingly, his own appreciation of our work and his thanks. The moment was impressive. Afterward General Longcroft came up to the Mess and chatted with the officers on the British theory of offensive in the air.

This letter, this little informal but very cordial address, and this simple quiet moment of relaxation, which the British know so well how to make significant, closed our career with the Royal Air Force.

On November 1st we entrained at the railhead at Saulty, proceeding in the usual box cars labelled "*8 chevaux—40 hommes*," to Candas, and thence, *via* Château Thierry and Châlons, to Toul. The five Fiat trucks with trailers and one motor side-car proceeded at the same time with twelve men and an officer, under the command of Lieutenant Wells, through Doullens, Amiens, Roye, Noyon, Château Thierry, and Châlons, to Toul. The squadron, on its arrival, was assigned to the Fourth Pursuit Group, under the command of Major Charles J. Biddle, and occupied, with the 25th, 141st, and 148th, the French cavalry barracks (*Casernement de Goncourt*) at Toul aerodrome, on the north side of the city. Spads were designated as the machines that we were to fly, but before we could get our full complement of them allotted to us and obtain even a part of the tools necessary for testing and tuning them up, before our pilots had even a chance to learn to fly them, the armistice was signed and active operations were over.

The 17th Squadron had, at the Front, a singularly happy career; and to that happiness, which diffused a unison through it and an intention all its own, it owed doubtless, in no small degree, its effectiveness. Imbedded in an allied army, concerning the inner workings of which it had neither interest nor knowledge, it waged war with a high sense

Good-bye to the British front

of simple duty uncontaminated by the obscure friction and ambi-
tions that so often paralyze action and create unfortunate situations
of strain, delay, and uncertainty. We asked for nothing but a chance to
show what American flyers could do with American soldiers standing
loyally behind them. We asked only to be allowed to be, in the fullest
sense of the words, a fighting unit. This opportunity the British gave
us to their utmost ability and in an unstinted measure that we might
otherwise never have known. They had nothing else that they could
give—neither advancement nor power.

And from us—there was no one among us who was more than a
mere subaltern—they could expect nothing but the quintessence of
an offensive spirit in the face of the common enemy. To afford that
spirit scope, and to that end alone, they put completely and unreserv-
edly at our disposal the great, simple, direct organization of the Royal
Air Force—an organization from which pretence, incoherence, and
lost motion had been largely burned away by the flame of four years'
tragic and indecisive warfare. They met us as man to man, in the great
task of defeating the enemy, with a direct cordiality that was a recognition of service in which no second thoughts and mental reserves could
play a part. They supported us eminently, and we lived and fought to
be not unworthy of the confidence they had come to repose in us. It
was a rare situation—never, perhaps, again to be presented.

CHAPTER 5

# Combat Reports

## 1

Pilot: Lieut. R. D. Williams.
Date: July 20, 1918.
Time: 9:45 a. m.
Locality: Near Ostend, two or three miles east.
Duty: Escort.
Height: 20000 down to 16000 feet.
Result: 1 Fokker destroyed; 1 Fokker driven down under control.
Our formation encountered five Fokker biplanes near Ostend. They were at about 21000 feet. We were at 20000, but fought down to 16000 or 17000. Fired several bursts at rather long range, 150-200 yards, at two different machines. One seemed to be hit as tracer bullet seemed to explode in fuselage back of pilot. He went down under control.
One other Fokker dove on me firing short burst. Manoeuvred so that I was only about twenty-five yards to his left rear, as he was making a slow climbing turn; gave him a burst of forty or fifty bullets which appeared to enter his machine at pilot's seat. He turned on his back and fell straight out of sight, apparently out of control.

(Sgd.) R. D. Williams.
Confirmed:                    (Sgd.) Samuel B. Eckert,
2 Section, 6 D.A., Belgian Army, 1st Lieut., A.S., Sig. R.C.,
through American Mission.    Commanding 17th Squadron.

## 2

Pilot: Lieut. R. M. Todd.
Date: August 1, 1918.
Time: 9:00 a. m.
Locality: near Provin.
Duty: Offensive Patrol.
Height: 14000 to 16000 feet.
Result: 1 Fokker triplane destroyed.
While on offensive patrol 8:00–10:00 a. m., August 1, 1918, our formation met three triplanes and one Fokker biplane at 14000 to 16000. The leading three of our formation dived on the E.A. and when the E.A. turned, I dove on the nearest triplane, opening fire at about 100 yards range. The triplane pulled up, allowing me to get within 25 yards of him, and my next burst sent him down out of control. While watching him, I went into a spin accidently and pulled out of it at about 6000 feet. While still diving, I saw the triplane crash into a wood near Provin (Hazebrouck SA, 1-100,000 C.K.). This was about 8:50–9:00 a. m.

|  | (Sgd.) Robert M. Todd. |
| --- | --- |
| Confirmed: | (Sgd.). Samuel B. Eckert, |
| R.A.F., *Communiqué*, | 1st Lieut. A.S., U.S.R., |
| No. 18, August 1, 1918. | Commanding 17th Squadron. |

## 3

Pilot: R. D. Gracie.
Date: August 1, 1918.
Time: 9:30 a. m.
Locality: Wytschaete.
Duty: Offensive Patrol.
Height: 15000 feet.
While on O.P., 8:00–10:00 a. m. met five Fokkers and a Pfalz at about 16000, at 9:30 a. m. between Wulverghem, Wytschaete, Messines and Hollebeke. Fired at one Fokker from below about 150 rounds at 200–300 yards. E.A. went into spin but I did not watch him for more than 2000 or 3000 feet as there were other E. A. still on top of me.

(Sgd.) Ralph D. Gracie.

Pilot: Lieut. M. K. Spidle.
Date: August 1, 1918.
Time: 9:33 a. m.
Locality: Between Messines and Hollebeke.
Duty: Offensive Patrol.
Height: 14000 feet.
While on O. P. our formation met three Fokker biplanes and one Fokker triplane at 14000 feet at 9:25-9:35 a. m., between Wulverghem, Wytschaete, Messines, and Hollebeke. Fired 150 rounds into Fokker biplane which spun 4000 feet and flattened out and then dived again. Did not see it crash.

(Sgd.) M. K. Spidle.

## 5

Pilot: Lieut. W. H. Shearman.
Date: August 1, 1918.
Time: 9:35 a. m.
Locality: Area between Wytschaete and Hollebeke.
Duty: Offensive Patrol.
Height: 14000-15000 feet.
Four E.A. seen about a thousand feet above our formation, 9:25-9:35 a. m., between Wytschaete, Wulverghem, Messines, and Hollebeke. We climbed to meet E.A. which when directly overhead, dived through formation. A Pfalz attacked right of our formation from sun, and came through formation, right to left, directly in front of my guns. My first burst struck front of machine slightly in advance of cockpit, and machine passed slightly under and to my left. I turned and dived putting a burst into the cockpit of E.A. The machine wavered, side-slipped slightly, went down in a dive. The E.A. was diving straight down and I followed him down until I was at 13000 feet, the enemy formation being then at 8000 feet, and the Pfalz at 3000 feet still going down, when I lost sight of him under the wing of my machine. The machine was diving directly toward our lines.

(Sgd.) W. H. Shearman.

## 6

Pilot: Lieut. W. J. Armstrong flying Sopwith Camel, D. 9499.
Date: August 3, 1918.

Time: 8:25 a. m.
Locality: South of Roulers.
Duty: Offensive Patrol.
Height: 12000 feet.
Result: 1 Fokker triplane destroyed.
While on offensive patrol, 7:30 to 9:30 a. m., August 3, 1918, I met a formation of Fokker biplanes and triplanes. Caught one triplane unawares at 8:30 a. m. and fired 50 rounds from thirty yards right into him at 12000 feet; saw tracers go straight into machine. I overshot and could not follow him down below 10000 feet. Location about one and a half miles south of Roulers.

(Sgd.) William J. Armstrong.
While on offensive patrol, 7:30-9:30 a. m., August 3, 1918, at 12000 feet, I saw an E.A. below me. I dived on this machine to 9000 feet but was unable to get within firing distance and flattened out. I then saw a Fokker triplane go in a steep spiral apparently out of control. I spiralled down to between 5000 and 6000 feet from whence I saw him crash in a vertical nose dive into the ground.

(Sgd.) W. H. Shearman.

| | |
|---|---|
| Confirmed: | (Sgd.) Samuel B. Eckert, |
| R. A. F., *Communiqué* | 1st Lieut., A.S., U. S. R., |
| No. 18, August 3, 1918. | Commanding 17th Squadron. |

## 7

Pilot: Lieut. M. L. Campbell.
Date: August 3, 1918.
Time: 8:30 a. m.
Locality: South of Roulers.
Duty: Offensive Patrol.
Height: 12000 feet.
Result: 1 Fokker biplane destroyed.
While on O.P., 9:30 a. m., August 3, 1918, I encountered a Fokker biplane at 12000 feet and dived on him following him down to 1000 feet firing about 400 rounds (closest range about 100 yards). Smoke appeared in the cockpit of E.A., at about 3000 feet but machine did not catch on fire. E.A. turned on his left wing tip and dived straight down into the ground. I saw him crash in the middle of a field of crops and I was then at

1000 feet so came straight back. Exact locality unknown on account of clouds. Heavy machine gun fire (white tracers) when returning, from roads about a mile from where E.A. was seen to crash.

(Sgd.) Merton L. Campbell.
Confirmed: (Sgd). Samuel B. Eckert,
R.A.F., *Communiqué*, 1st Lieut., A.S., U.S.R.,
No. 18, August 3, 1918. Commanding 17th Squadron.

## 8

Pilot: Lieut. L. A. Hamilton.
Date: August 7, 1918.
Time: 11:10 a. m.
Locality: Armentieres.
Duty: Offensive Patrol.
Height : 8000–500 feet.
Result: 1 Fokker biplane destroyed.
While on offensive patrol at 16000 feet we saw eight Fokker biplanes at 8000 feet over Armentieres. We dove, taking them by surprise. E.A. dove away from us. I settled on the tail of one Fokker and fired 200 rounds into him as he spiralled down to 8000 feet. I followed him down to 5000 feet at which point a cloud of black smoke issued from his cock-pit and he went down in an extremely steep spiral through a cloud, apparently out of control. When I came out of the cloud a Fokker fired at me head on. I climbed and turned on to his tail and fired at him following him down to about 3000 feet. As he dove away, Lieut. Campbell came in on the side and then on to his tail, firing several bursts. I saw E.A. crash into a green field just east of Armentieres. Lieut. Campbell was at about 100 feet and I was at 500, both getting badly machine gunned. When I was going toward the lines I saw another Fokker biplane badly crashed on the ground just east of Armentieres, in a trench.

(Sgd.) Lloyd A. Hamilton.
For Lieut. R. M. Todd's Statement, see Combat Report, No. 10.
Confirmed : R.A.F. *Communiqué*,
No. 19, August 7, 1918.

## 9

Pilot: R. W. Snoke.
Date: August 7, 1918.
Time: 11:20 a. m.
Locality: Armentières.
Duty: Offensive Patrol.
Height: 8000 feet.
Result: 1 Fokker biplane driven down.
While on offensive patrol at 16000, saw five Fokker biplanes at about 8000 feet. Dove and fired 100 rounds at one which I followed down to 3500 feet. White smoke appeared to come out of the E.A. which continued to go down in a steep spiral. At this point I turned to find another E.A. and lost sight of him.

(Sgd.) Ralph W. Snoke.

## 10

Pilot: M. L. Campbell.
Date: August 7, 1918.
Time: 11:30 a. m.
Locality: Armentières.
Duty: Offensive Patrol.
Height : 8000 feet.
Result: 2 Fokker biplanes destroyed.
1. While on an O.P. encountered a flight of five Fokker biplanes over Armentieres. After getting behind them and in the sun, we dove on them (E.A. being at about 8000 feet). Fired two bursts (about 75 rounds) into one after which he went down out of control, having turned over on his back. Other E.A. prevented me from watching him further at the time. Closest range forty yards.
2. Attacked another E.A. just west of Armentieres fired about eight bursts into him (175 rounds) and drove him down to the ground, last burst being at about 100 feet range. E.A. was seen to crash in green field, striking nose first. I went down to 100 feet from the ground. Machine gun fire from buildings when returning to our lines.

(Sgd.) Merton L. Campbell.

While on offensive patrol at 10:00–12:00 a. m. near Armentieres, ran into a formation of five E.A. (Fokker biplanes), at a height of about 6000 feet. We dove on them from about 9000 feet and four of them dove away from us. The fifth E.A. stayed in clouds and I stayed up with him while the rest of the formation went down after the four E.A. After two short bursts, the E.A. in clouds put his nose down and went into Hunland away from the fight. I returned and stayed above the fight at a height of about 5000 from whence saw two E.A. crash into field. About a minute later I saw a Camel after an E.A. very close to the ground. This E.A. also crashed immediately.

(Sgd.) Robert M. Todd.

(Sgd.) Lloyd A. Hamilton.

Confirmed:  (Sgd.) Samuel B. Eckert,

R.A.F., *Communiqué,*  1st Lieut. A.S., U.S.R.

No. 19, August 7, 1918.  Commanding 17th Squadron.

## 11

Pilot: Lieut. W. J. Armstrong.

Date: August 8, 1918.

Time: 9:35-9:45 a. m.

Locality: Between Zeebrugge and Knocke.

Duty: Covering Bombing Raid.

Height: 12000 feet.

While on offensive patrol, met six Fokker biplanes between Zeebrugge and Knocke, at 9:30, at 17000 feet. Three came down and we engaged them and drove them down. Then two more came down to our height—about 14000 feet. I engaged one of them and he went into a dive. I fired about 100 rounds into him from a range of fifty yards. My tracers were going right into him.

Something seemed to explode in his machine and he kept right on diving towards Het Zoute (5.N.6.) with smoke streaming out. I followed him down to 7000 feet when another Fokker got on my tail. I engaged him and he went down but levelled out over the sea.

(Sgd.) William J. Armstrong.

Indecisive.  (Sgd.) Samuel B. Eckert.

1st Lieut. A.S., Sig. R.C.,

Commanding 17th Squadron.

71

## 12

Pilot: Lieut. R. D. Williams.
Date: August 9, 1918.
Time : 8:40–8:45 a. m.
Locality: 1 mile south of Armentières.
Duty: Offensive Patrol.
Height: 7000 feet.
Result: 1 E.A. driven down out of control.
Remarks: Three scouts, apparently of new type with no over-hang and tails rather like Camels, short flat nose that looked like rotary motor, going north. Guns firing forward, speed about same as Camel. Performance not as good.

While on O.P. at 8:40–8:45 a. m. this date, I became separated from our formation, which was split up in fight near Lille, and while trying to overtake it I was cut off by three scouts which appeared about 400 feet above me. I turned and attacked leader and was immediately attacked by remaining two. After several minutes manoeuvring I succeeded in putting burst of thirty or forty into leader at about 50 or 75 yards. He fell in steep spiral nose dive but was not seen to crash. Continued fight with re-maining two, one of which fired burst of 100 rounds or more piercing my pressure tank. I switched on to gravity and dived zigzag for clouds which were at 3500 to 3000 feet. Crossed lines near Bailleul at 8:45.

(Sgd.) Rodney D. Williams.

While on O.P. at 8:40–8:45 this date, coming back from the en-gagement near Lille our formation was heavily archied, and one of our machines was left about a mile and a half behind. Three E.A. appeared on his left just south of Armentièes. He immedi-ately turned to attack them, employing chiefly a climbing right turn, and seemed to get on the tail of one of them, which I then saw fall in steep spiral nose dive and go below the clouds which were about 2500 feet. Shortly after this the Camel disappeared into the clouds in a series of sweeps from left to right, followed by the remaining two E.A. The fight started at 8:40–8:45, about 3000 feet which was the height of our formation.

(Sgd.) T. E. Tillinghast.

Indecisive.　　　　(Sgd.) Samuel B. Eckert,
　　　　　　　　　1st Lieut. A.S., Sig. R.C.,
　　　　　　　　　Commanding 17th Squadron.

## 13

Pilot: Lieut. W. H. Shearman.
Date: August 12, 191 8.
Time: 11:00 a. m.
Locality: Heyst.
Duty: Co-operation with Bombers.
Height: 15000 feet.
Result: 1 Fokker biplane destroyed.
Remarks: Fokker biplane camouflaged with broad irregular blotches of black and cream white.
While on O.P. cooperating with D.H.9 bombing squadron, two Fokker biplanes dove on rear D.H.9. We turned to meet them. As Fokker turned to fire on one of our formation, he passed below me and in opposite direction. I fired burst as he passed and swung around on his tail opening fire a second time at about fifty yards, my tracers going directly into E.A. Fired 130 rounds from this position at point-blank range. E.A. went into straight nose dive slowly revolving about its longitudinal axis until he disappeared into ground haze. I was at that time at about 10000 feet.

(Sgd.) W. H. Shearman.

While I was on offensive patrol I saw Lieutenant Shearman on tail of E.A. firing at point-blank range. The E.A. went down into left-hand stall and into a vertical dive slowly revolving. I followed him down to 7000 feet and he was still in vertical turning dive when he disappeared in ground mist.

(Sgd.) L. E. Case.

Decisive.

(Sgd.) Samuel B. Eckert,
1st Lieut. A.S., Sig. R.C.,
Commanding 17th Squadron.

## 14

Pilot: Lieut. M. L. Campbell.
Date: August 14, 1918.
Time: 11:25 a. m.
Locality: Bruges.
Duty: Co-operation.
Height: 14000 feet.
Result: 1 Fokker biplane destroyed.
While accompanying bombers over Bruges at about 11:30 we

were attacked by formation of E.A. from above. I attacked one E.A. firing about 50 rounds into him, shortest range about fifty feet. E.A. went over on his back and I did not see him again. Got two No. 3 stoppages just before E.A. went down. While trying to remedy stoppages two E.A. attacked me. They followed me from Bruges, west to the lines firing a large number of rounds. Crossed lines just off the ground where I got considerable machine gun fire.

(Sgd.) Merton L. Campbell.

While on same patrol saw Lieut. Campbell attack and directly after saw an E.A. falling on back in slow spiral.

(Sgd.) Frank A. Dixon.

While on patrol saw an E.A. falling on back in a slow spiral after being attacked by one of our machines.

(Sgd.) Lloyd A. Hamilton.

Pilots of 211 Squadron saw two E.A. shot down and crashed by Camels, of which this was probably one.

Decisive:                  (Sgd.) Samuel B. Eckert,
Letter, O.C. 65th Wing,      1st Lieut. A.S., Sig. R.C.,
R.A.F.,65-G-245,
October 15, 1918.          Commanding 17th Squadron.

**15**

Pilot: Lieut. G. D. Wicks.
Date: August 14, 1918.
Time: 11:30 a. m.
Locality: S.W. of Bruges.
Duty: Co-operation with D.H.9 Bombers.
Height: 14000 feet.
Result: 1 Fokker biplane destroyed.

While on patrol cooperating with bombers encountered flight of six Fokker biplanes and one monoplane. One dived on formation, turning into me from rear. I pulled round and fired about seventy-five rounds at fifty feet, closest range; saw tracers going into fuselage. E.A. went over my head and, without attempting to pull up, went straight into Camel machine behind me. Camel's tail smashed and E.A.'s left lower wing was torn off. Both machines went straight down flopping about.

(Sgd.) Glenn D. Wicks.

While on same patrol saw E.A. and Camel falling together. The

Camel had tail plane and fuselage broken and E.A. had one wing torn off.

(Sgd.) Frank A. Dixon.
(Sgd.) Jesse F. Campbell.

Decisive.                           (Sgd.) L. A. Hamilton.
Confirmed:                          (Sgd.) Samuel B. Eckert,
R.A.F. *Communiqué*,                1st Lieut. A.S., Sig. R.C.,
No. 20, August 14, 1918.            Commanding 17th Squadron.

## 16

Pilot: Lieut. R. M. Todd.
Date: August 15, 191 8.
Time: 4:30-4:35 p. m.
Locality: Dixmude.
Duty: Co-operation with Bombers.
Height: 12000-9000 feet.
Coming home from cooperation show with 211 Squadron from 3:00 p. m. to 5:00 p. m., I lost my leader who dove on Huns and tagged on to Bentley Camel "E" from 210 Squadron. We came home together at 12000 feet and as we were about to cross the lines above Dixmude at 4:50 a Fokker opened fire on us at a range of about fifty yards, taking us by surprise. We both turned to the right and went after the E.A., the Bentley getting in front shot at it. The E.A. pulled up vertically and Bentley went underneath him; E.A. stalled and went into nose dive. This brought him in my range of fire and I dove on him firing a continuous burst for 3000 feet at a distance of 50 yards to 100 yards. E.A. went underneath me and I lost sight of him and after pulling out of dive could not get sight of E.A. again. I was able to see my tracers going into the E.A. and the last seen of it the E.A. was going down at a terrific speed.

(Sgd.) Robert M. Todd.

## 17

Pilot: Lieut. W. D. Tipton flying Sopwith Camel, F. 2157.
Date: August 21, 1918.
Time: 12:50 p. m.
Locality: 57c. F.22.
Duty: O.P. Co-operating with No. 6 Squadron.
Height: 12000 feet.

Result: 1 Fokker biplane driven down.

At 12:50 p. m., at 57c. F.22, while leading O.P. cooperating with R.E.8's, attacked 8 Fokker biplanes who were about 1000 feet above me. I pulled nose up, fired at leader who dove down under me. I dove on him firing a good burst. He went into a spin, could not follow him down as two other E.A. attacked me. Then engaged three others pulling up my nose and firing from below. We then fought a rear-guard action, while returning, as E.A. persisted in attacking from above and behind us. Number of rounds fired, 350.

> (Sgd.) William D. Tipton.
> (Sgd.) Samuel B. Eckert,
> 1st Lieut. A.S., Sig. R.C.,
> Commanding 17th Squadron.

## 18

Pilot: Lieut. F. M. Showalter flying Sopwith Camel, F. 1964.
Date: August 21, 1918.
Time: 12:50 p. m.
Locality: 57c. F.22.
Duty: Offensive Patrol.
Height: 1000 feet.
Result: 1 Fokker biplane driven down.

While on O.P. cooperating with R.E.8's, first saw two E.A. passing 500 to 800 feet below. One Camel dived on second while I dived on first. Fired about 100 rounds at a distance of about 300 yards. E.A. immediately half rolled to the right and dived steeply. I followed him down about 1000 feet firing short bursts into him; left him going down in what appeared to be an uncontrolled spin.

> (Sgd.) F. M. Showalter.
> (Sgd.) Samuel B. Eckert,
> 1st Lieut. A.S., Sig. R.C.
> Commanding 17th Squadron.

## 19

Pilot: Lieut. L. A. Hamilton flying Sopwith Camel, D. 1940.
Date: August 21, 1918.
Time: 12:55 p. m.
Locality: 57c .L.5.

Duty: Co-operative Offensive Patrol.
Height: 12000–4000 feet.
Result: 1 Fokker biplane destroyed.
While on O.P. cooperating with No. 6 Squadron we saw nine Fokker biplanes in the distance and headed for them. Some dove away and I followed one. He banked around and as I opened fire on him he dove away. I got on his tail and from a distance of 10–20 yards fired 350 rounds into him during which time he did not turn. At 5000 feet he began to smoke and I pulled away from him at 4000 feet.

(Sgd.) L. A. Hamilton.

Lieut. R. M. Todd's Statement.

While on O.P. cooperating with No. 6 Squadron at 12:00–2:00 p. m., August 21, 1918, we attacked nine E.A. at a height of 12000 feet. I dove with Lieut. Hamilton on a Fokker biplane. He was within 25 yards of E.A. and followed it for about 5000 feet in this position. I pulled out at 5000 feet and while circling around I saw the E.A. crash to earth at 57c. L.5. Confirmed:

(Sgd.) S. B. Eckert,

R.A.F. *Communiqué*,          1st Lieut. A.S., Sig. R.C.,
No. 21, August 21, 1918.     Commanding 17th Squadron.

**20**

Pilot: Lieut. M. L. Campbell, flying Sopwith Camel, D. 1941.
Date: August 21, 1918.
Time: 1 p. m.
Locality: Cambrai.
Duty: Co-operative Offensive Patrol.
Height: 11000 feet.
Result: 1 Fokker biplane driven down.
While on a cooperative O.P. with R.E.8's. we met a flight of E.A.'s. I turned on the E.A. which was behind and above, fired a long burst into him after which he went down in a dive. I had to turn at the time to prevent stalling and lost sight of E.A. Fired about 125 rounds at a range of from 250 to 200 yards.

(Sgd.) Merton L. Campbell.

Lieut. A. J. Schneider's Statement.

While on the above mentioned patrol saw Lieut. Campbell fire on E.A. which stalled and appeared to go down in a side-slip dive; I lost sight of him.

(Sgd.) Samuel B. Eckert,
1st Lieut. A.S., S.R.C.,
Commanding 17th Squadron.

## 21

Pilot: Lieut. R. D. Williams flying Sopwith Camel, D. 6595.
Date: August 21, 1918.
Time: About 1 p. m.
Locality: 57c. F.22.
Duty: Offensive Patrol.
Height: 11 000 feet.
Result: 1 Fokker biplane driven down out of control 1 Fokker biplane driven down. While on O.P. and cooperating with R.E.8's we met 8 Fokker biplanes at one p. m., 57c. F.22; we attacked, our leader diving on first Fokker; two Fokkers got on leader's tail and I attacked the rear E.A. of the two. Put a burst of 30 or 40 rounds into him at a range of 75 yards. Fokker seemed to hesitate, stall, turn to the left, and go down very steeply. Dove on the tail of foremost Fokker who half rolled to the right and went down in steep dive with another Camel on his tail which followed him several thousand feet.

(Sgd.) R. D. Williams.
(Sgd.) Samuel B. Eckert,
1st Lieut. A.S., Sig. R.C.,
Commanding 17th Squadron.

## 22

Pilots: Lieut. L. A. Hamilton flying Sopwith Camel, D. 1940.
     Lieut. R. M. Todd flying Sopwith Camel, D. 9513.
Date: August 21, 1918.
Time: 6:45 p. m.
Locality: 57c. H.17.
Duty: Offensive Patrol.
Height: 2000 feet.
Result: 1 enemy kite balloon destroyed.
While on offensive patrol at about 6:45 p. m., Lieut. Todd and myself dove on E. Balloon at 2000 feet at 57c. H.17. I saw my Buckingham going into balloon. I saw observer jump and saw balloon burst into flames at about 200 feet from ground. I fired

about 300 rounds.

(Sgd.) Lloyd A. Hamilton.

Lieut. R. M. Todd's Statement.

While on offensive patrol at about 6:45 p. m., Lieut. Hamilton and myself dove on E. Balloon at 2000 feet at 57c. H.17. I saw my Buckingham going into balloon. I saw observer jump and saw balloon burst into flames at about 200 feet from ground. I fired about 300 rounds.

Lieut. J. F. Campbell's Statement.

I saw Lieut. Todd and Lieut. Hamilton fire into balloon and saw it burst into flames about 200 feet from ground.

| | |
|---|---|
| Confirmed: | (Sgd.) Samuel B. Eckert, |
| R.A.F. *Communiqué*, | 1st Lieut. A.S., Sig. R.C., |
| No. 21, August 21, 1918. | Commanding 17th Squadron. |

## 23

Pilot: Lieut. H. C. Knotts flying Sopwith Camel, D. 6513.
Date: August 21, 1918.
Time: 7:15 p. m.
Locality: Bapaume.
Duty: Offensive Patrol.
Height: 3000 feet.
Result: 1 Fokker biplane driven down.

While on O.P. met 8 Fokkers over Bapaume at 7:15. One dove at me from side and I turned and fired one burst as he went past and dived away.

(Sgd.) Howard C. Knotts.
(Sgd.) Samuel B. Eckert,
1st Lieut. A.S., Sig. R.C.,
Commanding 17th Squadron.

## 24

Pilot: Lieut. W. D. Tipton.
Date: August 22, 1918.
Time: 9:50 a. m.
Locality: 57c. H.22.
Duty: O.P. Cooperating with R.E.S's.
Height: 1000 feet.
Result: 1 kite balloon destroyed.

While on cooperative patrol with R.E.8's at 9:50, dove with

Lieut. Williams on E.K.B. at 57c. H. 22, at 1000 feet. Fired long burst up to within 25 yards of K.B. which ignited and went down in flames. 400 rounds fired.

(Sgd.) W. D. Tipton.

(Sgd.) R. D. Williams.

Statement by Lieuts. Hamilton, Campbell, Wise, and Wicks. While on O.P. co-operating with No. 6 Squadron saw Lieuts. Tipton and Williams dive on balloon and shoot at it at very close range; the balloon went down in flames.

Confirmed: (Sgd.) Samuel B. Eckert,

R.A.F. *Communiqué*, 1st Lieut. A.S., Sig. R.C.,

No. 21, August 22, 1918. Commanding 17th Squadron.

## 25

Pilot: Lieut. R. M. Todd flying Sopwith Camel, D. 9513.

Date: August 22, 1918.

Time: 10:00 a. m.

Locality: 57c. H.30.

Duty: Cooperation with R.E.8's.

Height : 7000-4000 feet.

Result: 1 Fokker biplane destroyed.

While on cooperative patrol with R.E.8 squadron, we started down on balloon near 57c. H.32. Five Fokker biplanes attacked us at a height of about 7000 feet, and as Lieut. Hamilton and I dove on one enemy aeroplane, another E.A. got on my tail; I half rolled and came out on tail of E.A. who was diving down. I followed E.A. for about 1500 feet firing about 100 rounds into it at a range of 50 yards. I then lost him, as we had been diving east, and did not try to find E.A. again but rejoined formation.

Lieut. W. D. Tipton's Statement.

After attacking E.A., saw machine burning on ground in neighbourhood of 57c. H. 25-26-31-32.

Destroyed: "America."

Confirmed: (Sgd.) Samuel B. Eckert,

Letter, CO. 13th Wing, R.A.F., 1st Lieut. A.S., Sig. R.C.,

13 WP 54 October 12, 1918. Commanding 17th Squadron.

## 26

Pilot: Lieut. G. T. Wise flying Sopwith Camel, F. 9983.

Date: August 22, 1918.

Time: 10:00 a. m.

Locality: 57c. H.28.

Duty: Co-operative Offensive Patrol.

Height : 6000 feet.

Result: 1 Fokker biplane driven down out of control.

While on patrol co-operating with R.E.8's at 57c. H.28, 10:00 a. m., one Fokker biplane dove head on; I fired at point-blank range giving E.A. good burst. E.A. pulled into stall and fell out sideways, going down on side, in side-slipping dive. Could not observe result as two E.A. were firing from behind.

> Out of control, "America."
> (Sgd.) Samuel B. Eckert,
> 1st Lieut. A.S., Sig. R.C.,
> Commanding 17th Squadron.

## 27

Pilot: Lieut. L. A. Hamilton flying Sopwith Camel, D. 1941.

Date: August 22, 1918.

Time: 10:00 a. m.

Locality: 57c. H.30.

Duty: Co-operative Offensive Patrol. Height: 6000-1500 feet.

Result: 1 Fokker biplane driven down.

While on co-operative patrol with R.E. 8's, I got on to tail of Fokker who was firing at a Camel in our formation and followed him to 1500 feet. I shot 100 rounds into him with apparently no effect and then both of my guns jammed. Last seen going east at 500 feet under control.

> Driven down: "America."
> (Sgd.) Samuel B. Eckert,
> 1st Lieut. A.S., Sig. R.C.,
> Commanding 17th Squadron.

## 28

Pilots: Lieut. L. A. Hamilton flying Sopwith Camel, D. 1940.
  Lieut. J. F. Campbell flying Sopwith Camel, D. 6513.

Date: August 24, 1918.

Time: 2:10 p. m.

Locality: 57c. I.34.

Duty: Low Bombing.

Height: 1000 feet.

Result: 1 kite balloon destroyed.

While on low bombing east of Bapaume in company with Lieut. Hamilton, we attacked an enemy balloon at about 1000 feet. I fired 150 rounds at close range and balloon burst into flames and went down. I saw Lieut. Hamilton firing all the way down at close range on it.

### Remarks.

Lieut. Hamilton did not return from patrol and was seen by Lieut. Campbell, as above, apparently out of control near the balloon.

(Sgd.) J. F. Campbell.

| | |
|---|---|
| Confirmed: | (Sgd.) Samuel B. Eckert, |
| R.A.F. *Communiqué*, | 1st Lieut. A.S., S.R.C., |
| No. 21, August 24, 1918. | Commanding 17th Squadron. |

### 29

Pilot: Lieut. H. C. Knotts flying Sopwith Camel, B. 5428.
Date: August 25, 1918.
Time: 5:50 p. m.
Locality: Cambrai-Bapaume road, 57c. H.24.d.
Duty: Offensive Patrol.
Height: 2000 feet.
Result: 1 Fokker biplane destroyed.

While on offensive patrol, east of Bapaume, I lost my formation and stayed out over lines at about 2000 feet. Overhead was a flight of 148 U.S. Squadron. An E.A. diving away from them came in front of me. I got on his tail and fired about two bursts at a distance of about 10 to 20 yards. The E.A. fell, struck the ground, and burst into flames at 57c. H.24.d. I flew over the spot later and saw the E.A. burning on ground. About the time of my combat I saw an E.A. shot down by a member 148 U. S. Squadron, slightly above me. E.A. spun into ground and crashed. I saw it afterward on ground about 300 yards from where mine was burning. I got on the tail of another E.A. but my guns jammed, so came back home.

(Sgd.) H. C. Knotts.
Destroyed: "America."

| | |
|---|---|
| Confirmed: | (Sgd) Samuel B. Eckert, |
| R.A.F. *Communiqué*, | 1st Lieut. A.S., Sig. R.C., |
| No. 21, August 25, 1918. | Commanding 17th Squadron. |

Pilots: Lieut. R. M. Todd flying Sopwith Camel, D. 6595.

Lieut. W. D. Tipton flying Sopwith Camel, F. 5951.

Date: August 26, 1918.

Time: 5:00 p. m.

Locality: 57c. D.15.

Duty: Offensive Patrol.

Height: 1000 feet.

Result: 3 Fokker biplanes destroyed.

From Squadron Record Book, August 27, 191 8.

"On crossing lines 5 Fokkers were seen climbing about E. of Quéant (57c. D.15) at 5 p. m. Immediately afterwards one Camel was seen being attacked by 5 Fokkers in question at about 57c. B., at 1000 feet. The patrol at once went down to the assistance of this Camel and attacked the 5 Fokkers. Several other flights of Fokkers were then seen coming down from 6000. A general engagement occurred in which two other separate flights of Fokkers came down from higher up."

From post card from Lieut. W. D. Tipton,
forwarded from Aviation Officer,

35 Eaton Place, London, S. W. 1.

Was brought down in fight on August 26th in which I added 2 E.A. to my score; wounded slightly in both legs and petrol tank shot through. Todd, unwounded prisoner; Frost, severely wounded; Wise, unwounded prisoner; also Curtis and Ellis. Todd got one in scrap.

(Sgd.) W. D. Tipton.

Confirmed: R.A.F., 3rd Brig., 3 E.A. Destroyed: "America."

C.R.A.F., 2259-1 G.,          (Sgd.) S. B. Eckert,

November 6, 1918.          1st Lieut. Commanding.

**31**

Pilot: Lieut. R. W. Snoke flying Sopwith Camel, C. 8337.

Date: August 26, 1918.

Time: 5:05 p. m. .

Locality: 57c. E.16-10.

Duty: Offensive Patrol.

Height : 3000-5000 feet.

Result: 1 Fokker biplane driven down out of control.

While on offensive patrol I dived on three Fokkers; got on side of one which was diving on Camel; fired one hundred rounds at about 10 yards into him between his tail and wing. E.A. went down flopping about. I saw my tracers going into his cockpit. I was then attacked by from five to nine more E.A. from above, so came back to the lines, and picked up two other of our machines. As one of my centre section struts and right inter-wing struts were badly shot, I came home. I saw one E.A. crash at 57c. E.

> (Sgd.) R. W. Snoke.
> 1 E.A. Out of Control: "America."
> (Sgd.) Samuel B. Eckert,
> 1st Lieut. A.S., Sig. R.C.,
> Commanding 17th Squadron.

### 32

Pilot: Lieut. W. W. Goodnow flying Sopwith Camel, B. 7407.
Date: August 26, 1918.
Time: 5:05 p. m.
Locality: 57c. E.
Duty: Offensive Patrol.
Height: 5000 feet.
Result: 1 Fokker biplane driven down.
While on offensive patrol, formation was attacked by a large bunch of Fokkers. I stalled up and fired one short burst into one above me. He dived. I jumped on his tail; fired a good burst at 25 yards range. Another E.A. got on my tail; I turned under him and dove under another, turned under another and met another E.A. head on. Fired a good burst into him at point-blank range and zoomed over him. I could not see effect of my fire on any one of these, as three more E.A. got above and behind me and followed me back to the lines.

> (Sgd.) W. W. Goodnow.
> Indecisive: "America."
> (Sgd.) Samuel B. Eckert,
> 1st Lieut. A.S., Sig. R.C.
> Commanding 17th Squadron.

### 33

Pilot: Lieut. F. A. Dixon flying Sopwith Camel, B. 9263.

Date: August 26, 1918.
Time: 5:05 p.m.
Locality: 57c. E.
Duty : Offensive Patrol.
Heights: 5000-3000 feet.
Result: 2 Fokker biplanes destroyed.
1. While on offensive patrol our formation was attacked by numerous E.A. (Fokkers) one E.A. went in front of me; I fired 150 rounds; E.A. went over on his back and fell down smoking.
2. Another E.A. was following a Camel down; I got on E.A.'s tail, fired 50 rounds at a distance of 25 yards. The E.A. dived into the ground.

(Sgd.) F.A.Dixon.

Lieut. W. W. Goodnow's Statement.

1. I saw one E.A. go down in flames about 5:10 p. m. at about 57c. E.
2. I saw one E.A. crash at about 5:10 p. m. at 57c. E.

2 E.A. destroyed: "America."

| | |
|---|---|
| Confirmed: | (Sgd.) S. B. Eckert, |
| R.A.F. *Communiqué*, | 1st Lieut. A.S., Sig. R.C., |
| No. 22, August 25, 1918. | Commanding 17th Squadron. |

**34**

Pilot: Lieut. H. C. Knotts flying Sopwith Camel, B. 7896.
Date: September 13, 191 8.
Time: 6:45-6:50 p. m.
Locality: 57c. E.2.d.
Duty: Offensive Patrol.
Height: 4000 feet.
Result:1 Fokker biplane driven down out of control.
While on O.P. at 4000 feet at 57c. E.2.d., at 6:45-6:50 p. m., I saw two Fokker biplanes, one of which attacked an R.E.8. across the lines. He then turned back over the lines when the formation attacked the second E.A. and turning down fired at the formation from long range. I then made a climbing turn which put me on a level of and in the rear of E.A. who was still firing at the formation. I immediately opened fire at about 80 yards. E.A. turned over on his back and spun down in wide circles still on his back until out of sight at about 500 feet.

(Sgd.) Howard C. Knotts.

Confirmed:                          (Sgd.) Samuel B. Eckert,
R.A.F. *Communiqué*,                1st Lieut. U.S.A.S.,
No. 25, Sept. 16, 1918.             Commanding 17th Squadron.

## 35

Pilots: Lieut. W. T. Clements flying Sopwith Camel, F. 5993.
    Lieut. H. C. Knotts flying Sopwith Camel, F. 6308.
Date: September 17, 1918.
Time: 6:45 p. m.
Locality: 51b. R.14.a.
Duty: Offensive Patrol.
Height: 4000 feet.
Result: 1 Fokker biplane destroyed.
While on O.P. over Arleux we were attacked by a formation of
E.A., 11 of whom came down leaving 6 above us. In the dog-
fight which followed we fired on 1 E.A. with white tail and half
of fuselage painted white, about 50 rounds, each from the side,
at a range of about 100 to 75 yards.
On account of greater numbers attacking, the E.A. was im-
mediately lost sight of, but same machine identified by painting
was later seen by Lieut. Knotts crashed at about 51b. E.14.a.
                    (Sgd.) William T. Clements.
                    (Sgd.) Howard C. Knotts.
                    1 E.A. Destroyed: "America."
Confirmed:                          (Sgd.) Samuel B. Eckert,
R.A.F. *Communiqué*,                1st Lieut. U.S.A.S.,
No. 25, Sept. 17, 1918.             Commanding 17th Squadron.

## 36

Pilot: Lieut. H. Burdick flying Sopwith Camel, F. 2141.
Date: September 18, 1918.
Time: About 11:00 a. m.
Locality: 57b. G.11.
Duty: Offensive Patrol answering wireless calls.
Height: 1000 to 1500 feet.
Result: 1 L.V.G. destroyed.
While answering call R 99, 2 E.A. 80. IW, our patrol of 3 ma-
chines found 2 two-seaters at 4000 feet at about 11:00 a.m. but
not at the location indicated. We chased them down through
low clouds and then waited above for them to come back. As

they came up through the clouds, I attacked one of them, a L.V.G., diving on him, on his left side, at 1000 to 1500 feet, and opening fire at 50 yards range. The observer was seen to be shot and stopped firing. A few seconds later the machine burst into flames, and fell on 57b. G11.

(Sgd.) Howard Burdick.
1 E.A. in flames: "America."

Confirmed:           (Sgd.) Samuel B. Eckert,

R.A.F. *Communiqué,*      1st Lieut. U.S.A.S.,

No. 25, Sept. 18, 1918.     Commanding 17th Squadron.

## 37

Pilot: Lieut. G. A. Vaughn flying Sopwith Camel, F. 6034.
Date: September 18, 1918.
Time: About 11:00 a. m.
Locality: 57b. G.10 (Rumilly).
Duty: Offensive Patrol answering wireless calls.
Height: 1000 to 1500 feet.
Result: 1 L.V.G. driven down.
While answering call R 99, 2 E.A. 80. IW, our patrol of 3 machines found two L.V.G.'s at 11:00 a. m., but not where call pinpointed them. They dived through clouds at our approach, and came back west. We met them again as they came up through clouds. Lieut. Wicks and myself put a number of bursts directly into one of them. I saw the observer crumple up in the cockpit and cease firing. The machine, that was then under 1000 feet, went into a steep dive over Rumilly (57b. G.10), Heavy machine gun fire from the ground prevented further observation.

(Sgd.) G. A. Vaughn.
(Sgd.) G. D. Wicks.
(Sgd.) Samuel B. Eckert,
1st Lieut. U. S. A. S.,
Commanding 17th Squadron.

## 38

Pilot: Lieut. G. D. Wicks flying Sopwith Camel, F. 5967.
Date: September 22, 1918.
Time: 8:45 a. m.
Locality: 57b. G.13; west of Rumilly.
Duty: Offensive Patrol.

Height: 2000–3000 feet.

Result: 1 Fokker biplane destroyed.

While on O.P. at 8:45 a. m., a formation of about 18 E.A. (who were reinforced by more during the fight which followed) seemed to dive on "C" flight of our formation. Our flight dived into the fight. I dived on to one E.A. who was above the rest, and followed him in a wide half-circle down to the ground firing about 100 rounds at an average range of 100 yards. E.A. seemed to be falling out of control and just at last tried to straighten out and land but crashed.

(Sgd.) Glenn D. Wicks.

I saw this machine completely crashed on ground at 57b. G.13.

(Sgd.) Howard C. Knotts.
1 E.A. destroyed: "America."

Confirmed:  (Sgd.) Samuel B. Eckert,
R.A.F. *Communiqué*,  1st Lieut. U. S. A. S.,
No. 25, Sept. 22, 1918.  Commanding 17th Squadron.

## 39

Pilot: Lieut. G. A. Vaughn flying Sopwith Camel, F. 6034.

Date: September 22, 1918.

Time: 8:45–8:55 a. m.

Locality: Southwest of Cambrai.

Duty: Offensive Patrol.

Height : About 6000 feet.

Result: 1 Fokker biplane destroyed.

While on offensive patrol at 8:45 a.m., I dived vertically on E.A. which was circling over machine of our formation at 7000–8000 feet and fired at him from a range of 50 yards. He dived steeply past others of our machines below, and I could not observe results, since I turned to engage another E.A. which I shot down and which was observed to crash by Lieut. Dixon (See Combat Report 9. 22s).

(Sgd.) G. A. Vaughn.

While on offensive patrol about 8:45–8:55 a. m., I dived on Fokker biplane that came down from among several of our machines who were fighting just above me and, just as he passed me and I was about to fire on him, he burst into flames and went down southwest of Cambrai.

88

(Sgd.) Frank A. Dixon.
1 E.A. destroyed: "America."
Confirmed:                          (Sgd.) Samuel B. Eckert,
R.A.F. *Communiqué*,                1st Lieut. U. S. A. S.,
No. 25, Sept. 22, 1918.                Commanding 17th Squadron.

## 40

Pilot: Lieut. G. A. Vaughn flying Sopwith Camel, F. 6034.
Date: September 22, 1918.
Time: 8:45 a. m.
Locality: S.E. of Fontaine-Notre-Dame.
Duty: Offensive Patrol.
Height: About 7000 feet.
Result: 1 Fokker biplane destroyed.
While on offensive patrol about 8:45 a. m., I saw about 15 to 18 Fokkers coming down, as it seemed to me, from 15000 feet, over Rumllly, on our "C" flight formation. I dived to 7000-8000 into fight with my formation and got on the tail of one E.A., firing a good burst into him at 50 yards or less, from behind and above. He went down in side–slips and steep dives out of control. I followed him down to about 2000 feet, but could not see him crash because of many E.A. attacking me, the original E.A. formation having been re-enforced.
(Sgd.) G. A. Vaughn.
I saw this machine (E.A.) crash, at 57c. F.22, S.E. of Fontaine-Notre-Dame.

(Sgd.) Frank A. Dixon.
1 E.A. destroyed: "America."
Confirmed:                          (Sgd.) Samuel B. Eckert,
R.A.F. *Communiqué*,                1st Lieut. U. S. A. S.,
No. 25, Sept. 22, 1918.             Commanding 17th Squadron.

## 41

Pilot: Lieut. H. C. Knotts flying Sopwith Camel, B. 7896.
Date: September 22, 1918.
Time: 9:10 a. m.
Locality: 51b. W.22.
Duty: Offensive Patrol.
Height: 6000 feet.
Result: 1 Fokker biplane destroyed.

While on offensive patrol about 9:10 a. m., Lieut. Clements and myself dived on one of two E.A. below us. E.A. came around under me trying to escape Lieut. Clements; I fired about 300 rounds, at an average range of about 20 yards. Saw pilot throw up his hands as though he had been hit, but he apparently regained control again and tried to land, but before he could make landing he turned over on his back and crashed into edge of wood, at 51. W.22.a. where I saw him later hanging upside down in trees.

(Sgd.) Howard C. Knotts.

I saw this E.A. crashed in wood, south of Cambrai, near intersection of canal and road, at 51b. W.22.c.

(Sgd.) Albert J. Schneider.
1 E.A. destroyed: "America."

Confirmed:                (Sgd.) Samuel B. Eckert,
R.A.F. *Communiqué*,         1st Lieut. U. S. A. S.,
No. 25, Sept. 22, 1918.     Commanding 17th Squadron.

## 42

Pilots: Lieut. W. T. Clements flying Sopwith Camel, F. 5993.
Lieut. J. F. Campbell flying Sopwith Camel, F. 2146.
Date: September 22, 191 8.
Time: 9 :40 a. m.
Locality: Over Inchy.
Duty: Offensive Patrol.
Height: 8000 feet.
Result: Indecisive. While on O.P., 9 :40 a. m., about 8000 feet over Inchy, my flight
attacked a Halberstadt two-seater and I followed up firing about 75 rounds. We followed him into Hunland about 2 miles and then left him on approach of a formation of Fokkers. No effect of our fire was observed.

(Sgd.) W.T. Clements.

I fired one burst into above two-seater. No effect observed. We left him on approach of a formation of Fokkers.

(Sgd.) J. F. Campbell.
Indecisive: "America."
(Sgd.) Samuel B. Eckert,
1st Lieut. U. S.A. S.,
Commanding 17th Squadron.

90

Pilot: Lieut. H. C. Knotts flying Sopwith Camel, B. 7896.
Date: September 24, 1918.
Time: 10:40 a.m.
Locality: 57c. F.1.a. (Coupez Mill).
Duty: Offensive Patrol.
Height: 6000 feet.
Result: 2 Fokker biplanes destroyed.
While on O.P., at 6000 feet, about 10:40 a. m., we were attacked by a formation of eight E.A. who were apparently diving at our lower flight. Lieut. Clements went after one. I went after another, but saw an E.A. with a green tail and red fuselage get on Lieut. Clements' tail. I immediately turned from the E.A. I was diving on and attacked the one on Lieut. Clements' tail. I fired a long burst of about 100 rounds, at about 40 to 50 yards range. He went straight down to the ground and crashed at 57c. F.1.a. (Coupez Mill).
While on the same patrol as above, I turned back west to pick up my formation and was fired on from the rear by another E.A. with a white tail. I turned back and got on his tail. At my first burst he burst into flames. While turning I saw four more E.A. right on top of me. I dove and turned toward the lines and came directly back as I was having trouble with my guns. The four E.A. followed me to the lines.

|  | (Sgd.) H. C. Knotts. |
|---|---|
|  | 2 E.A. destroyed: "America." |
| Confirmed: | (Sgd.) Samuel B. Eckert, |
| R.A.F. *Communiqué*, | 1st Lieut. U. S. A. S., |
| No. 26, Sept. 24, 1918. | Commanding 17th Squadron. |

## 44

Pilot: Lieut. L. J. Desson flying Sopwith Camel, H. 7272.
Date: September 24, 191 8.
Time: 10:40 a.m.
Locality: 57c. J-P.
Duty: Offensive Patrol.
Height: 5000-6000 feet.
Result: 1 Fokker biplane driven down. While on offensive patrol, I attacked an E.A. (Fokker), getting in two bursts of 75 rounds, at 20 yards, after getting on his tail. I saw my tracers

going directly into the cockpit of the machine. E.A. went down apparently under control. I could not observe results on account of the many Fokkers attacking at that moment.

(Sgd.) Lieut. L. J. Desson.
(Sgd.) Samuel B. Eckert,
1st Lieut. U. S.A. S.,
Commanding 17th Squadron.

## 45

Pilot: Lieut. W. T. Clements flying Sopwith Camel, F. 5993.
Date: September 24, 191 8.
Time: 10:40 a. m.
Locality: 57c. E.27.b.
Duty: Offensive Patrol.
Height: 6000 feet.
Result: 1 Fokker biplane destroyed.
While on offensive patrol, at 13000 feet, at about 10:40 a. m., eight Fokkers started diving, apparently on our lowest formation. We followed them down, catching them at about 5000 to 6000 feet. In fight which followed I got on one Fokker's tail, firing about 150 rounds, at an average range of about 50 yards. My last burst went directly into him while he was in a vertical bank. He went into a vertical side-slip, and I pulled out on account of other E.A. being close on to my tail. At this time I was at about 1000 feet. Within a few minutes I saw a Fokker at his back right under me, on. the ground at 57c. E.27 b.1-1.

(Sgd.) W. T. Clements.
1 E.A. destroyed: "America."
Confirmed:        (Sgd.) Samuel B. Eckert,
R.A.F. *Communiqué*,    1st Lieut. U.S.A.S.,
No. 26, Sept. 24, 1918.    Commanding 17th Squadron.

## 46

Pilot: Lieut. J. F. Campbell flying Sopwith Camel, F. 2146.
Date: September 24, 1918.
Time: 10:40 a. m.
Locality: 57c. K.27.
Duty: Offensive Patrol.
Height: 6000 feet.
Result: 1 Fokker biplane driven down out of control.

While on offensive patrol, at 13000 feet, about 10:40 a. m. I saw eight Fokkers diving, apparently on our lower flight. We followed, and I got on E.A.'s tail and followed him from about 8000 feet to 3000 firing about 125 rounds, at an average range of 50 yards. My last burst I saw go directly into cockpit. He turned over on his back and went down in a slow flat spin still on his back. More E.A. prevented me from seeing him crash. This was practically over Havrincourt village (57c. K.27).

(Sgd.) J. F. Campbell.

I saw the E.A. crashed by Lieut. J. F. Campbell, at 3:50 p. m. at 57c. K.27.

| Confirmed: | (Sgd.) H. C. Knotts. |
|---|---|
| Letter 13 WP. 54, | (Sgd.) Samuel B. Eckert, |
| October 12, 1918. | 1st Lieut. U. S. A. S., |
| C.O. 13th Wing, R.A.F. | Commanding 17th Squadron. |

## 47

Pilot: Lieut. W.W. Goodnow flying Sopwith Camel, C. 8352.
Date: September 24, 1918.
Time: 10:45 a. m.
Locality: N.W. of Havrincourt.
Duty: Offensive Patrol.
Height: 7000 feet.
Result: 1 Fokker biplane driven down.
While on offensive patrol, I fired 50 rounds at 7000 feet, at 50 yards, head on at a Fokker biplane that was diving on Lieut. Donoho's machine. Result not observed on account of general engagement.

(Sgd.) W.W. Goodnow.
(Sgd.) Samuel B. Eckert,
1st Lieut. U. S. A. S.,
Commanding 17th Squadron.

## 48

Pilot: Lieut. G. A. Vaughn flying Sopwith Camel, F. 2146.
Date: September 24, 1918.
Time: 10:45-10:55 a. m.
Locality: 57c. P-Q. Duty: Offensive Patrol.
Height: 4000 feet.
Result: 1 Fokker biplane driven down.

I saw a Fokker chasing a Camel and shot a couple of bursts of 100 rounds at him, at 4000 feet, at 50 yards range from the side. He spun down. Was attacked from behind, turned and fired 50 rounds, at 75 yards, at second E.A. who half rolled and dived east. I chased him, but he out-dived me.

(Sgd.) Lieut. G. A. Vaughn.
(Sgd.) Samuel B. Eckert,
1st. Lieut. U. S. A. S.,
Commanding 17th Squadron.

## 49

Pilot: Lieut. H. Burdick flying Sopwith Camel; F. 2141.
Date: September 24, 1918.
Time: 10:50 a. m.
Locality: N.W. of Havrincourt (57c. J.23).
Duty: Offensive Patrol.
Height: 5000 feet.
Result: 1 Fokker biplane destroyed.
While on O.P., I saw a Fokker biplane dive at Lieut. Dixon at 5000 feet, N.W. of Havrincourt Wood, at 10:50 a. m. Lieut. Dixon half rolled and Fokker pulled up and half rolled. I half rolled and fired a burst of 100 rounds into him, at 25 yards range, from directly behind. He turned on his back and continued to spin on his back down over 57c. J.23.

(Sgd.) H. Burdick.
At 10:55 a. m. I saw a Fokker lying on its back at 57c. J.23.
(Sgd.) John A. Myers.
1 E.A. destroyed: "America."

Confirmed:          (Sgd.) Samuel B. Eckert,
R.A.F. *Communiqué*,    1st Lieut. U. S. A. S.,
No. 26, Sept. 24, 1918.    Commanding 17th Squadron.

## 50

Pilot: Lieut. J. F. Donoho flying Sopwith Camel, C. 3351.
Date: September 24, 1918.
Time: 10:45 a. m.
Locality: 57c J and P.
Duty: Offensive Patrol.
Height: 7000 feet.
Result: 1 Fokker biplane driven down. While on offensive pa-

trol I engaged a Fokker head on, at 7000 feet, at 10:45, firing a burst of 25 rounds into him, at 15 yards range. No results observed an account of many Fokkers diving down and firing all around me.

> (Sgd.) John F. Donoho.
> (Sgd.) Samuel B. Eckert,
> 1st Lieut. U. S. A. S.,
> Commanding 17th Squadron.

## 51

Pilot: Lieut. A. J. Schneider flying Sopwith Camel, F. 6024.
Date: September 24, 191 8.
Time: 10:50 a. m.
Locality: Over Havrincourt Wood.
Duty: Offensive Patrol.
Height: 5000-500 feet.
Result: 1 Fokker biplane driven down out of control.
While on O.P., at about 10:50 a. m., over Havrincourt Wood, I followed a Fokker biplane down to about 500 feet; got in several bursts of about 75 rounds, at about 50 to 75 yards, having got on his tail. He turned on his back, righted himself, and turned on his back again, falling toward 57c. J. and P. I could not follow him to ground because of turning against a Fokker that attacked an S. E. 5 that was driving another Fokker down. S.E. landed west of Havrincourt Wood (57c. P.3.) and turned over on his back. This was about 10:55 a. m.

> (Sgd.) Albert J. Schneider.
> (Sgd.) Samuel B. Eckert,
> 1st Lieut. U. S. A. S.,
> Commanding 17th Squadron.

## 52

Pilot: Lieut. J. F. Campbell flying Sopwith Camel, F. 2146.
Date: September 27, 1918.
Time: 5:35 p. m.
Locality: 57b. C.15.
Duty: Offensive and Bombing Patrol.
Height: 5000 to 2500 feet.
Result: 1 Fokker biplane driven down out of control. While on O.P., at 5:35 p. m., at about 5000 feet, I saw an E.A. under

clouds. I dived on him and followed him down to about 2500 feet, firing about 50 rounds; closest range about 75 yards. E.A. half rolled and went down in a slow spin; did not follow him any lower as a large formation of E.A. was above us, coming down.

(Sgd.) J, F. Campbell.

I saw the Fokker biplane attacked by Lieut. Campbell in a slow spin about 100 feet from the ground at 57b. C.15. My attention was drawn away by E.A. coming down from above so did not see him crash.

(Sgd.) C. W. France.
(Sgd.) Samuel B. Eckert,
1st Lieut. U. S. A. S.,
Commanding 17th Squadron.

## 53

Pilot: Lieut. H. Burdick flying Sopwith Camel, F. 2141.
Date: September 28, 1918.
Time: (1) 5:45 p. m. (2) 6:10 p. m.
Locality: (1) 51a.T.7.d. (2) 51b. X.12.d.
Duty: Offensive and Bombing Patrol.
Height: (1) 3000 feet (2) 500 feet.
Result: 2 Fokkers destroyed.

While on offensive and bombing patrol, about 5:45 p. m., at 3000 feet, I went down on an E.A. two-seater (L.V.G.), from in front of him, and was attacked by two Fokkers. I manoeuvred, got on their tails, shot about 100 rounds into one, range about 25 yards. He burst into flames at about 1500 feet (51a.T.7.d.). Fired about 50 rounds into other Fokker with no apparent result. Left him going east and returned to lines.

Saw three Fokkers diving on Lieut. Wicks, at 6:10 p. m., about 500 feet. I fired about 25 rounds from long range; one E.A. left going east; I closed in and half rolled on to tail of one, with red nose, white tail, which was diving on Lieut. Wicks. Fired about 50 rounds, at 50 yards. He dove straight into ground, at 51b. X.12.d.

(Sgd.) Howard Burdick.

I saw a Fokker biplane, with red nose and white tail, lying on his back on ground, at 51b. X.12.

(Sgd.) H. P. Alderman.

I saw a Fokker, with red nose and white tail, on his back at 51b. X.12.

(Sgd.) Frank A. Dixon.
2 E.A. destroyed: "America."

Confirmed:           (Sgd.) Samuel B. Eckert,
R.A.F. *Communiqué*      1st Lieut. U. S. A. S.,
No. 26, Sept. 26, 1918.     Commanding 17th Squadron.

## 54

Pilot: Lieut. G. A. Vaughn flying Sopwith Camel, H. 828.
Date: September 28, 1918.
Time: 5:45 p. m.
Locality: 51a. T.7.
Duty: Offensive and Bombing Patrol.
Height: 3000 feet.
Result: 1 L.V.G. two-seater destroyed.
While on offensive and bombing patrol 5:40-5:45 p. m., dived on an L.V.G. two-seater, firing a number of good bursts from less than 50 yards from behind, following him down, from 3000 to 100 feet, over 51a. M.34. I saw him last diving vertical into ground, at which moment I was attacked by seven Fokkers.

(Sgd.) G. A. Vaughn.

I saw Lieut. Vaughn, at 5:40-5:45 p. m., follow this E.A. down to less than 50 feet, at which height the two-seater was diving directly into ground. Could not see him crash being attacked by two Fokkers.

(Sgd.) Howard Burdick.

I saw this two-seater diving into ground, at less than 50 feet, when the formation was attacked by Fokkers.

(Sgd.) Frank A. Dixon.

This L.V.G. two-seater was diving directly into ground, under 50 feet, when I last saw him, at about 5:45 p. m., when I was attacked by Fokkers and broke the leading edge of my lower right- hand plane on upper branches of a tree.

(Sgd.) Glenn D. Wicks.
1 two-seater E.A. (L.V.G.)
destroyed: "America."

Confirmed: Letter 13 WP. 54,   (Sgd.) Samuel B. Eckert,
October 12, 1918,         1st Lieut. U. S. A. S.,
C.O. 13th Wing, R.A.F.     Commanding 17th Squadron.

## 55

Pilot: Lieut. F. A. Dixon flying Sopwith Camel, F. 6183. «
Date: September 28, 1918.
Time: 5:45 p. m.
Locality: 51b. X.12.
Duty: Offensive and Bombing Patrol.
Height: 3000 feet.
Result: 1 Fokker biplane driven down. While on offensive and bombing patrol, at 5:45 p. m., seven Fokkers came down at our formation. As I was above our formation, one came at me. I pulled up and fired 30 rounds and dove. Fokker did not follow, stopped firing and turned east,

(Sgd.) Frank A. Dixon.
(Sgd.) Samuel B. Eckert,
1st Lieut. U. S. A. S.,
Commanding 17th Squadron.

## 56

Pilots: Lieut. G. A. Vaughn flying Sopwith Camel, H. 828.
     Lieut. H. Burdick flying Sopwith Camel, F. 2141.
Date: October 2, 1918.
Time: 9:10 a. m.
Locality: East of Awoingt (57b. B. 23.).
Duty: Offensive and Bombing Patrol.
Height: 3500 feet.
Result: 1 D. F. W. two-seater destroyed.
While on O.P., immediately after dropping bombs on Awoingt, saw 2 two-seaters, at 3500 feet, at 9:10 a. m., just E. of Awoingt. Fired at them and they dived east. Lieut. Burdick and I followed one D. F. W., with orange fuselage and camouflaged wings, and shot him down attacking first from the front. I got in 150 rounds from 75 yards. He went down in half-dive, half-spin, and crashed into the ground at 57b. B. 23.

(Sgd.) G. A. Vaughn.

While on O.P., we dropped bombs from 3000 feet, on Awoingt, at 9:10 a. m., and immediately saw 2 two-seaters slightly above us just to east of Awoingt. Lieut. Vaughn and I engaged one of them, a D. F. W., and shot him down, firing about 150 rounds from 75 yards or under. He crashed into the ground at 57b. B. 23.

(Sgd). Howard Burdick.

I saw this D.F.W., shot down by Lieuts. Vaughn and Burdick, crash at 57b. B. 23.

(Sgd.) G. D. Wicks.

Lieuts. Vaughn and Burdick attacked a D.F.W. just east of Awoingt and shot him down. I saw him crash at 57b. B.23., a few minutes after 9:10 a. m.

(Sgd.) Frank A. Dixon.

1 E. A. destroyed: "America."

Confirmed:     (Sgd.) Samuel B. Eckert,

R.A.F. *Communiqué*,     1st Lieut. U. S. A. S.,

No. 27, October 2, 1918.     Commanding 17th Squadron.

## 57

Pilots: Lieut. G. A. Vaughn flying Sopwith Camel, H. 828.

Lieut. H. Burdick flying Sopwith Camel, H. 830.

Date: October 14, 1918.

Time: 7:10 a. m.

Locality: E. of Bazuel (57a. M.22.).

Duty: Special Bombing Raid.

Height: 1500 feet.

Result: 1 Halberstadt two-seater destroyed.

While on special bombing raid, on October 14th, at 7:10 a. m., saw 2 two-seaters just east of Bazuel (57a. R.8) at 1500 feet, a Halberstadt and an L.V.G., which, after dropping our bombs on Bazuel, Lieut. Burdick and I attacked, firing 200 rounds from 75-100 yards at Halberstadt and sending it down.

(Sgd.) G. A. Vaughn.

While on special bombing raid, on October 14, at 7:10 a. m., saw 2 two-seaters, at 57a. R.8., to the east of Bazuel, at 1500 feet. Lieut. Vaughn and I attacked a Halberstadt. I fired 100 rounds from 75-100 yards and saw it crash at about 7:12 a. m., at 57a. M.22.a. L.V.G. got away north.

(Sgd.) Howard Burdick.

1 E.A. destroyed: "America."

Confirmed:     (Sgd.) Samuel B. Eckert,

R.A.F. *Communiqué*,     1st Lieut. U. S. A. S.,

No. 29, October 14, 1918.     Commanding 17th Squadron.

## 58

Pilots: Lieut. G. A. Vaughn flying Sopwith Camel, H. 828.

Lieut. J. A. Myers flying Sopwith Camel, F. 2007.

Lieut. H. Burdick flying Sopwith Camel, H. 830.

Date: October 14, 1918.

Time: 2:00 p. m.

Duty: Offensive and Bombing Patrol.

Height: From 2500 feet to ground.

Result: 1 Fokker biplane destroyed.

While on low bombing patrol, at 51a. Q.23, a Fokker biplane came in front of formation in a spin. In front of me it flattened out and I fired a short burst. E.A. went into spin, flattened out near ground and landed.

> (Sgd.) G. A. Vaughn.

I fired one burst into E.A., as above.

> (Sgd.) J. A. Myers.

While on offensive and low bombing patrol, at 2:00 p. m. near Hausey (northeast), saw a Fokker spinning down among our formation. I fired about 50 rounds from 25 yards at him and followed him down. E.A. landed successfully at 51a. Q.25. Pilot got out and started to run across field. I dove on him and fired at him from about 5 or 10 feet from ground and very close. He fell in the field about 100 yards from the machine (west) and was lying there when I left. I fired my remaining ammunition at the Fokker trying to set it on fire.

> (Sgd.) Howard Burdick.

Confirmed: (                    Sgd.) Samuel B. Eckert,

G.H.Q., R.A.F.,              1st Lieut., U. S. A. S.,

October 14, 1918.          Commanding 17th Squadron.

## 59

Pilot: Lieut. H. Burdick flying Sopwith Camel, H. 830.

Date: October 25, 1918.

Time: 10:55 a. m.

Duty: Offensive Patrol.

Locality: Near Mormal Forest.

Height : 7000 feet.

Result: 1 Fokker biplane in flames.

While on O.P., I left formation at 10:50 a. m., and attacked leading E.A. of a formation of five Fokker biplanes at 7000 feet that were going N.W., somewhere near Mormal Forest (impossible to see the ground). I fired about 40 rounds at 75 yards, diving on him from the front and immediately pulled up in a climbing turn and went west to rejoin my formation. I saw the Fokker fall out of control, start to spin, and burst into flames after he had spun down about 1000 feet.

(Sgd.) Howard Burdick.

1 E.A. destroyed: "America."

Confirmed:              (Sgd.) Weston W. Goodnow.

G.H.Q., R.A.F.,          1st Lieut. U.S.A.S.,

October 25, 1918.        Commanding 17th Squadron.

# CHAPTER 6

# Report of Low Bombing and Machine Gun Attack on Varssenaere Aerodrome

Dawn: August 13, 1918.

Lieut. Lloyd A. Hamilton: Dropped four bombs on north hangars from about 200 feet, shot fifty rounds into the windows of the *château*, made four circuits of the field shooting at a row of five Fokkers on the ground with engines running up. On first circuit shot first enemy machine in this line and saw it burst into flames, on third circuit shot third enemy machine in the line and saw it burst into flames.

Lieut. Robert M. Todd: Dropped four bombs from 250 feet on *château*, fired a number of rounds into the *chateau* and at machines and personnel on the ground. Saw northeast hangars blazing; saw seven enemy machines burning on the ground.

Lieut. Albert J. Schneider: Dropped two bombs on hangars and two on machine gun emplacements from about 250 feet and shot pilot getting into one of the Fokkers lined up on the aerodrome.

Lieut. William H. Shearman: Dropped four bombs from about 200 feet on buildings, apparently billets, to the east of hangars; saw bombs burst and the buildings start to smoke; shot down man on his way to machine gun; shot one burst into one of a row of four enemy machines on the ground and saw tracers going directly into hood of the engine; shot into barracks and on way home at the crew of the anti-aircraft gun to the west of the aerodrome.

Lieut. Floyd M. Showalter: Dropped four bombs on hangars from about 200 feet; fired 600 rounds into *château*, hangars, and anti-aircraft batteries on the way home.

Lieut. Weston W. Goodnow: Dropped four bombs from about 200 feet on machine shops which were afterwards seen to be burning; shot into a row of machines on the ground, two were already burning; smoke came from third afterwards.

Lieut. George T. Wise: Dropped four bombs from about 200 feet on machine shops. Three machines were burning on the ground; one other beginning to burn. Saw shops on fire; made three trips around the aerodrome shooting at enemy machines on the ground and into hangars.

Lieut. Merton L. Campbell: Dropped four bombs into north hangars from about 200 feet; machine gunned *château* and enemy machines on the ground; machine gunned anti-aircraft batteries on the way home.

Lieut. Lyman E. Case: Dropped four bombs on machine shops from about 200 feet; shot 400 rounds into enemy machines on ground; saw two Fokkers destroyed by fire and one struck by bomb; saw fires on northeast side of aerodrome.

Lieut. Leonard J. Desson: Dropped four bombs on *château* from about 300 feet and fired into windows; was compelled to climb as air pressure was dead and had to depend on gravity and hand pump.

Lieut. Frank A. Dixon: Lost patrol and being unable to locate it dropped four bombs on Ostend from 6000 feet.

Lieut. Rodney D. Williams: Returned at 5:10 a. m. with broken connecting rods.

## 1

17th Squadron, U.S.A.

No. and type of machines:
Sopwith Camels, F 2157,
D. 6595, F. 5967, B. 9263.

No. 1–23, page 1.

Date: August 23, 1918.

Locality: 57c.S.7.b.

Lieut. W. D. Tipton.
Sopwith Camel, F. 2157.

Dropped 1 bomb at 1:10 P. M. near stationary transport, about 12 lorries on road between Bazentin-le-Petit and Martinpuich; fired about 600 rounds at transport at about 200 feet.

Lieut. R. D. Williams.
Sopwith Camel, D. 6595.

Dropped 3 bombs on same road. Dropped bomb near and fired about 400 rounds into gun pit, at about 57c. S.7.b., at about 200 feet.

Lieut. F. A. Dixon.
Sopwith Camel, F. 5967.

3 bombs near transport between Bazentin-le-Petit and Martinpuich; fired about 200 rounds into same transport.

Lieut. G. D. Wicks.
Sopwith Camel, B. 9263.

Dropped 4 bombs on transport of about 25 horse and motor vehicles moving towards lines on road between Bazentin-le-Petit and Flers. Fired about 400 rounds; saw drivers and horses scattering in the fields.

## 2

17th Squadron, U.S.A.

No. and type of machines:
Sopwith Camels, D. 1940,
D. 9399, D. 6513, B. 5428.

No. 2–23, page 1.

Date: August 23, 1918.

Locality: Martinpuich—Le Barque and Courcellette—Bapaume roads.

Lieut. L. A. Hamilton.
Sopwith Camel, D. 1940.

At 2 P. M. dropped 4 bombs on long transport, probably 25 to 30 horse-drawn vehicles, on Martinpuich—Le Barque Road, 57c.M. 28 and 27. Shot about 600 rounds into them. Saw at least two direct hits and at least two vehicles destroyed and many dead horses, others scattering.    Transport going toward Bapaume.

Lieut. J. F. Campbell.    At 2 P. M. dropped 4 bombs as above
Sopwith Camel, D. 6513.    and shot 600 rounds into transport.
Lieut. A. J. Schneider.    At 2 P. M. dropped 4 bombs on trans-
Sopwith Camel, B. 5428.    port Courcellette—Bapaume Road, fir-
ing about 600 rounds.

Lieut. R. M. Todd. .    At 2 P. M. dropped 4 bombs on balloon
Sopwith Camel, D. 9399.    on ground at 57c.N.31.    Shot at trans-
port on Martinpuich—Le Barque Road and machine gunned driver running to ditch and killed him.    Attacked machine gun emplacement on same road, killing both gunners and putting machine gun out of action.    Flying at 50 to 100 feet, saw many dead horses.


Remarks.

Saw many enemy troops proceeding toward Bapaume in side roads.   Le Transloy—Bapaume and Flers—Ligny-Thilloy roads and Albert—Bapaume road very little traffic.


3

17th Squadron, U.S.A.    No. 3-23, page 1.
No. and type of machines:    Date: August 23, 1918.
Sopwith Camels, B. 7407,    Locality: Bapaume road
C. 8337, F. 1964, F. 2164.    through Le Transloy.

Lieut. W. W. Goodnow.    Time: 5:50 P. M.    Dropped 4–20 lb.
Sopwith Camel, B. 7407.    bombs on 8 lorries halted at meeting of 4 roads at 57c.N.24.    Saw hits, and bombs of rest of flight drop in and about transport and personnel.    Fired 500 rounds from about 1000 feet at transport and personnel.

Lieut. F. M. Showalter.    Time: 5:50 P. M.    Dropped 3–20 lb.
Sopwith Camel, F. 1964.    bombs from 1000 feet in and about transport at same spot as above.    Saw bombs drop beside road and in ditches,

fired at transport and personnel. Fired a number of rounds at a balloon on ground at 57c.N.24.c.

Lieut. G. T. Wise. Sopwith Camel, F. 2164.
Time: 5:50 P. M. Dropped 3–20 lb. bombs on same transport as above and one bomb on hut, at 57c.N.30.c., which was seen to burn. Dived on about a half a company of infantry on side-road near by, scattering them. Then attacked a machine gun emplacement by Eaucourt, firing about 200 rounds.

Lieut. R. W. Snoke. Sopwith Camel, C. 8337.
Time: 5:50 P. M. Dropped 4–20 lb. bombs on five lorries at cross-roads, 57c.N.25.c. Saw one bomb drop between two lorries. Guns jammed; flew away; cleared guns; came back and machine gunned four lorries remaining, firing about 500 rounds.

### Remarks.

On account of severe machine gun fire from the ground and smoke and dusk from bombs bursting, could not observe amount of damage done but would consider it quite extensive as these hits on transports were all practically direct.

### 4

17th Squadron, U.S.A.
No. and type of machines:
Sopwith Camels, F. 2157, D. 6595, F. 5967, B. 9263.

No. 4-23, page 1.
Date: August 23, 1918.
Locality: S.W. of Bapaume.

Lieut. W. D. Tipton. Sopwith Camel, F. 2157.
Time: 6:45 P. M. Dropped 4–20 lb. bombs from 500 feet on 6 lorries on road S.W. of Bapaume, 57c.M.31 and 32. Saw bombs burst among transport and 1 lorry blown over on side. 14 Fokkers above Bapaume uniting to come down.

Lieut. R. D. Williams. Sopwith Camel, D. 6595.
Landed at aerodrome at No. 3 Squadron, R.A.F. Wounded in back by bul-

let through petrol tank; came all the way back with finger in hole of petrol tank. Was seen by Lieut. Tipton shooting at transport from 100 feet; apparently dropped bombs at same spot.

Lieut. G. D. Wicks.
Sopwith Camel, F. 5967.

Had forced landing near Auxi-le-Château just after taking off. Crashed; pilot unhurt (engine trouble).

Lieut. F. A. Dixon.
Sopwith Camel, B. 9263.

Time: 6:45 P. M. Dropped 4–20 lb. bombs on same transport; fired 200 rounds from 1000 feet. Saw Lieut. Tipton's and some of Lieut. Williams' drop in and about the lorries. Saw Lieut. Tipton's bomb overturn a lorry.

Remarks.

Practically all bombs were direct hits on this transport; one lorry was destroyed and others apparently damaged; much confusion was noticed among personnel. Very little troop movement noticed; all transport moving N.E. Lieut. Williams in C.C.S., Gézaincourt.

**5**

17th Squadron, U.S.A.
No. and type of machines:
Sopwith Camels, D. 1940,
D. 6513, C. 141, D. 8337,
F. 5985.

No. 1a-24, page 1.
Date: August 24, 1918.

Lieut. L. A. Hamilton.
Sopwith Camel, D. 1940.
Time: 2:10 P. M.
Height: 1000 feet.
Rounds fired: unknown.
Bombs dropped 4–20 lb.

Bombs on hut and transport at 57c. I.20. With Lieut. Campbell destroyed a balloon at 57c.I.34. Did not return; last seen out of control by Lieut. Campbell.

Lieut. J. F. Campbell.
Sopwith Camel, D. 6513.
Time: 2:10 P. M.
Height: 1000 feet.
Rounds fired: 200.
Bombs dropped: 4–20 lb.

Dropped 4 bombs on same hut as above. Fired with Lieut. Hamilton on balloon. Saw it burst into flames and go down.

Lieut. H. B. Frost.
Sopwith Camel, C. 141.
Time: 2:25 P. M.
Height: 1500 feet.
Rounds fired: 200.
Bombs dropped: 4–20 lb.

Bombs on transport at fork by town of Quéant (57c.d.28) going east—about 40 lorries densely packed. Bombs fell among lorries. Saw E.A. on ground, 51b.S.23.b.

Lieut. A. J. Schneider.
Sopwith Camel, D. 6513.
Time: 3:00 P. M.
Height: 1500 feet.
Rounds fired: unknown.
Bombs dropped: 4–20 lb.

Bombs dropped between railroad and road at Vaulx Vraucourt. Got one direct hit and saw another burst near train apparently loading or unloading. Saw about a battalion of infantry and what appeared to be two tanks S.W. of Bapaume.

Lieut. R. W. Snoke.
Sopwith Camel, C. 8337.
Time: 3:20 P. M.
Height: 1000 feet.
Rounds fired: 400.
Bombs dropped: 4–20 lb.

Bombs dropped on guns going west at 57c.C.18. Shot at small body of troops accompanying guns. Men scattered. Shot at one balloon on ground and one off ground, 57c.B.24. Could not see effect.

Lieut. G. T. Wise.
Sopwith Camel, F. 5985.
Time: 3:20 P. M.

Not returned from patrol at 5:25 P. M.

**6**

17th Squadron, U.S.A.
No. and type of machines:
Sopwith Camels, F. 1964,
B. 7407.

No. 1a-24.
Date: August 24, 1918.
Locality: Bapaume-Cambrai Road, 57c.H.30.

Lieut. W. W. Goodnow.
Sopwith Camel, B. 7407.
Time: 3:15 P. M.
Height: 1000 feet.
Rounds fired: 200.
Bombs dropped: 4–20 lb.

Dropped 4 bombs on isolated transport, Bapaume—Cambrai Road, 57c.-H.30. Dropped beside it. Fired 200 rounds on balloon on ground at 57c.-H.22.

Lieut. F. M. Showalter.
Sopwith Camel, F. 1964.
Time: 3:15 P. M.
Height: 1000 feet.
Rounds fired: 300.

Dropped 4 bombs on same transport. Did not see effect. Fired 300 rounds into transport after most of it had stopped.

Bombs dropped: 4–20 lb.

## 7

17th Squadron, U.S.A.
No. and type of machines:
Sopwith Camels, C. 8337,
F. 1964.

No. 2a-24.
Date: August 24, 1918.
Locality: 57c.N.30.

Lieut. R. W. Snoke.
Sopwith Camel, C. 8337.
Time: 6:30 P. M.
Height: 1000 feet.
Rounds fired: 500.
Bombs dropped, 4–20 lb.

4 bombs on cross road; one burst near transport and one among transport. Other two unseen. Saw transport and troops on road to the south. Fired 300 rounds from 800 feet at them. They scattered and saw many fall. Horses on road to the north. Shot 150 rounds into them. Transport moving east greatly congested, both horse and lorry.

Lieut. F. M. Showalter.
Sopwith Camel, F. 1964.
Time: 6:30 P. M.
Height: 1000 feet.
Rounds fired: nil.
Bombs dropped: 4–20 lb.

Dropped bombs on horse and motor transport going east and southeast near Le Transloy.

## 8

17th Squadron, U.S.A.
No. and type of machines:
Sopwith Camels, F. 2157,
F. 1950.

No. 2a-24, page 1.
Date: August 24, 1918.
Locality: Bancourt—Haplincourt and Bapaume—Cambrai roads.

Lieut. W. D. Tipton.
Sopwith Camel, F. 2157.
Time: 7:10 P. M.
Height: 1200 feet.
Rounds fired: 500.
Bombs dropped, 1–20 lb.

Fifty lorries in groups of 6 to 12 moving southeast between Bancourt and Haplincourt. Dropped 1 bomb on a line of 12. Four stopped apparently hit and others went around. All traffic moving east and southeast.

Lieut. G. D. Wicks.
Sopwith Camel, F. 1950.
Time: 7:10 P. M.

Saw bombs burst among same transport as above. Three big guns moving toward Cambrai at 7:20 P. M., ref:

Height: 1200.                     57c.J.8 and 9. Many lorries on Ba-
Rounds fired: 400.                paume and Cambrai road. Dived on
Bombs dropped: 1–20 lb.           some of these firing about 200 rounds.
                                  Fired 200 rounds at the guns.


## 9

17th Squadron, U.S.A.             No. 2a-24.
No. and type of machines:         Date: August 24, 1918.
Sopwith Camels, F. 2164,          Locality: Vaulx-Vraucourt.
B. 9263.


Lieut. R. M. Todd.                Dropped bombs on town of Vaulx
Sopwith Camel, F. 2164.           Vraucourt. Seven Fokkers, two two-
Time: 7:45 P. M.                  seaters above. Returned home at 1000
Height: 3000 feet.                feet.
Rounds fired: 300.
Bombs dropped: 4–20 lb.

Lieut. F. A. Dixon.               Dropped 2 bombs at 57c.28.b. and 2
Sopwith Camel, B. 9263.           at 57c.26.b. on transport on road, mov-
Time: 7:45 P. M.                  ing east. Fired 200 rounds at trans-
Height: 1500 feet.                port. Saw 7 Fokkers overhead. Saw
Rounds fired: 200.                Camel marked "24" before national
Bombs dropped: 4–20 lb.           marking, "N" behind, fire bursts at
                                  57c.36.b. and saw burst on ground and
                                  fire—evidently result of Camel's fire.

### Remarks.

Very little enemy aërial activity marked early part of the day.
Considerable, however, in the afternoon. Traffic on roads quite
congested and all moving east and southeast.

## 10

17th Squadron, U.S.A.             Date: September 24, 1918.
No. and type of machine:          Locality: Bapaume—Cam-
Sopwith Camel, B. 7896.           brai road.

Lieut. H. C. Knotts.              Saw 500 troops and two lorries on
Sopwith Camel, B. 7896.           Bapaume—Cambrai road, coming west
Time: 3:50 P. M.                  at 3:50. Went down to 800–900 feet,
Height: 800–900 feet.             fired at them, hit ammunition dump,
Rounds fired: 100.                by the side of road (57c.E.29.a.) which

Bombs dropped: nil.

exploded. This explosion was seen from A.L.G. by a ground officer of 59 Squadron; also seen by Lieut. Springs, 148th Squadron, U.S.A.

## 11

17th Squadron, U.S.A.
No. and type of machines:
Sopwith Camels, H. 828,
H. 7272, F. 5967, F. 2141,
F. 6138, C. 8352, C. 3351,
F. 2142, F. 5993, F. 2146,
D. 3396, D. 9423, F. 6024,
C. 8337.

No. 3a-27-s.
Date: September 27, 1918.
Locality: 57c. F. 13-14-15.

Lieut. G. A. Vaughn.
Sopwith Camel, H. 828.
Time: 10:45 A. M.
Height: 2500 feet.
Rounds fired: nil.
Bombs dropped: 4–20 lb.

Dropped bombs on Fontaine-Notre-Dame.

Lieut. L. J. Desson.
Sopwith Camel, H. 7272.
Time: 10:45 A. M.
Height: 2500 feet.
Rounds fired: nil.
Bombs dropped: 4–20 lb.

"          "          "

Lieut. G. D. Wicks.
Sopwith Camel, F. 5967.
Time: 10:45 A. M.
Height: 2500 feet.
Rounds fired: nil.
Bombs dropped: 4–20 lb.

Dropped bombs near Bourlon Wood.

Lieut. H. Burdick.
Sopwith Camel, F. 2141.
Time: 10:45 A. M.
Height: 2500 feet.
Rounds fired: nil.

"          "          "

Bombs dropped: 4–20 lb.


Lieut. F. A. Dixon.        "       "       "
Sopwith Camel, F. 6138.
Time: 10:45 A. M.
Height: 2500 feet.
Rounds fired, nil.
Bombs dropped: 4–20 lb.

Lieut. W. W. Goodnow.    Dropped bombs near Bourlon Wood.
Sopwith Camel, C. 8352.
Time: 10:45 A. M.
Height: 2500 feet.
Rounds fired: nil.
Bombs dropped: 4–20 lb.


Lieut. J. F. Donoho.       "       "       "
Sopwith Camel, C. 3351.
Time: 10:45 A. M.
Height: 2500 feet.
Rounds fired: nil.
Bombs dropped: 4–20 lb.


Lieut. W. L. France.       "       "       "
Sopwith Camel, F. 2142.
Time: 10:45 A. M.
Height: 2500 feet.
Rounds fired: nil.
Bombs dropped: 4–20 lb.


Lieut. W. T. Clements.      "       "       "
Sopwith Camel, F. 5993.
Time: 10:45 A. M.
Height: 3000 feet.
Rounds fired: nil.
Bombs dropped: 4–20 lb.


Lieut. J. F. Campbell.       "       "       "
Sopwith Camel, F. 2146.

Time: 10:45 A. M.
Height: 3000 feet.
Rounds fired: nil.
Bombs dropped: 2–20 lb.

Lieut. M. C. Giesecke.        Dropped bombs near Bapaume—Cam-
Sopwith Camel, D. 3396.    brai road.
Time: 11:00 A. M.
Height: 3000 feet.
Rounds fired: nil.
Bombs dropped: 2–20 lb.

Major H. L. Fowler.           Dropped bombs on main road just
Sopwith Camel, D. 9423.    west of Fontaine-Notre-Dame.
Time: 10:45 A. M.
Height: 2500 feet.
Rounds fired: nil.
Bombs dropped: 2–20 lb.

Lieut. A. J. Schneider.        Dropped bombs near Bourlon Wood.
Sopwith Camel, F. 6024.
Time: 10:45 A. M.
Height: 2500 feet.
Rounds fired: nil.
Bombs dropped: 2–20 lb.

Lieut. J. A. Myers.            Dropped bomb near Bourlon Wood.
Sopwith Camel, C. 8337.
Time: 10:45 A. M.
Height: 2500 feet.
Rounds fired: nil.
Bombs dropped: 1–20 lb.

## 12

17th Squadron, U. S. A.        No. 4a-27-s.
No. and type of machines:    Date: September 27, 1918.
Sopwith Camels, F. 5993,     Locality: Canal de l'Escaut
F. 2146, F. 6024, D. 3396,    at Marcoing.
H. 828, F. 5967, F. 2141,
F. 6138, F. 6194, F. 2164,
C. 8397, F. 6211, C. 3351,
H. 7272.

| | | |
|---|---|---|
| Lieut. W. W. Goodnow.<br>Sopwith Camel, F. 2164.<br>Time: 4:30 P. M.<br>Height: 2500 feet.<br>Rounds fired: nil.<br>Bombs dropped: 4–20 lb. | Dropped bombs on troops on approach to bridge over Canal de l'Escaut at Marcoing. | |
| Lieut. J. A. Myers.<br>Sopwith Camel, C. 8337. | " " " | |
| Lieut. F. M. Showalter.<br>Sopwith Camel, F. 6211. | " " " | |
| Lieut. J. F. Donoho.<br>Sopwith Camel, C. 3351. | " " " | |
| Lieut. L. J. Desson.<br>Sopwith Camel, H. 7272. | " " " | |
| Lieut. G. A. Vaughn.<br>Sopwith Camel, H. 828. | " " " | |
| Lieut. G. D. Wicks.<br>Sopwith Camel, F. 5967. | " " " | |
| Lieut. H. Burdick.<br>Sopwith Camel, F. 2141. | " " " | |
| Lieut. F. A. Dixon.<br>Sopwith Camel, F. 6138. | " " " | |
| Lieut. C. W. France.<br>Sopwith Camel, F. 6194. | " " " | |
| Lieut. W. T. Clements.<br>Sopwith Camel, F. 5993. | " " " | |
| Lieut. J. F. Campbell.<br>Sopwith Camel, F. 2146. | " " " | |
| Lieut. A. J. Schneider,<br>Sopwith Camel, F. 6024. | " " " | |
| Lieut. M. C. Giesecke.<br>Sopwith Camel, B. 3396. | " " " | |

## 13

| | |
|---|---|
| 17th Squadron, U. S. A.<br>No. and type of machines:<br>Sopwith Camels, F. 6024,<br>H. 828, F. 2141, F. 6249. | No. 5a-28-s.<br>Date: September 28, 1918.<br>Locality: Naves and Cambrai. |

114

Lieut. A. J. Schneider. Dropped bombs on Naves, 57a.T.23.
Sopwith Camel, F. 6024. Fired 200 rounds on Naves and 200
Time: 5:00 to 8:50 A. M. rounds on lorries in main square, Cam-
Height: 3000 feet. brai, from 3000 feet, at 8:00 A. M.
Rounds fired: 400. One enemy balloon, east of Cambrai,
Bombs dropped: 4–20 lb. about 500 feet high.

Lieut. G. A. Vaughn. Four bombs on Faubourg de Paris.
Sopwith Camel, H. 828.
Time: 6:40 A. M.
Height: 3000 feet.
Rounds fired: nil.
Bombs dropped: 4–20 lb.

Lieut. H. Burdick.              "              "              "
Sopwith Camel, F. 2141.
Time: 5:00–5:30 A. M.
Height: 3000 feet.
Rounds fired: nil.
Bombs dropped: 4–20 lb.

Lieut. E. D. White.              "              "              "
Sopwith Camel, F. 6249.
Time: 5:00–5:30 A. M.
Height: 3000 feet.
Rounds fired: nil.
Bombs dropped: 1–20 lb.

## 14

17th Squadron, U.S.A. No. 5b-28-s.
No. and type of machines: Date: September 28, 1918.
Sopwith Camels, C. 8352, Locality: Rumilly.
F. 2142, F. 6211, H. 7272,
H. 828, F. 5967, F. 2141,
F. 6138, F. 6249, F. 2164,
F. 5993, F. 2146, H. 7281,
F. 6024, D. 3396.

Lieut. W. W. Goodnow. Four bombs on balloon. No effects
Sopwith Camel, C. 8352. observed. Railway bridge, at 57b.
Time: 4:55 P. M. A.9-b, seen to burst into white smoke
Height: 2000 feet. on the Cambrai end, at 5:10 P. M.
Rounds fired: nil.

Bombs dropped: 4–20 lb.

Lieut. J. F. Donoho.
Sopwith Camel, F. 6211.
Time: 5:10 P. M.
Height: 3500–800 feet.
Rounds fired: 150.
Bombs dropped: 4–20 lb.

Dropped two bombs on balloon from 3500 feet, at 4:55 P. M., 57b.G.18. Two bombs on Awoingt from 2500 feet, at 5:10 P. M. Fired 150 rounds at railway station, 57b.B.20, at 5:10, from 800 feet. Train passing came to a stop.

Lieut. W. T. Clements.
Sopwith Camel, F. 5993.
Time: 5:10–5:15 P. M.
Height: 3000–2000 feet.
Rounds fired: 300.
Bombs dropped: 4–20 lb.

Four bombs on Awoingt from 3000 feet, at 5:10 P. M. Fired 300 rounds on road S.E. of Cambrai, from 2000 feet, at 5:15 P. M. Heavy machine gun and AA fire from ground.

Lieut. J. A. Myers.
Sopwith Camel, F. 2164.
Time: 5:10–5:15 P. M.
Height: 3000–2000 feet.
Rounds fired: 300.
Bombs dropped: 4–20 lb.

"          "          "

Lieut. J. F. Campbell.
Sopwith Camel, F. 2146.
Time: 5:10–5:15 P. M.
Height: 3000–2000 feet.
Rounds fired: 250.
Bombs dropped: 4–20 lb.

Four bombs on Awoingt from 3000 feet, at 5:10 P. M. Fired 300 rounds on road S.E. of Cambrai, from 2000 feet, at 5:15 P. M. Heavy machine gun and AA fire from ground.

Lieut. A. J. Schneider.
Sopwith Camel, F. 6024.
Time:5:10–5:15 P. M.
Height: 3000–2000 feet.
Rounds fired: 100.
Bombs dropped: 4–20 lb.

"          "          "

Lieut. M. C. Giesecke.
Sopwith Camel, D. 3396.
Time: 5:10–5:15 P. M.
Height: 3000–2000 feet.
Rounds fired: 100.

"          "          "

Bombs dropped: 4–20 lb.


Lieut. H. P. Alderman.                "          "     ·     "
Sopwith Camel, H. 7281.
Time: 5:10–5:15 P. M.
Height: 3000–2000 feet.
Rounds fired: 500.
Bombs dropped: 4–20 lb.


| Lieut. G. D. Wicks. | Four bombs on road S.E. of Cambrai. |
|---|---|
| Sopwith Camel, F. 5967. | Fired 300 rounds into moving traffic on |
| Time: 5:00–5:30 P. M. | the Masnières—Cambrai road, just out- |
| Height: 2000–1000 feet. | side Cambrai and on other roads in this |
| Rounds fired: 300. | vicinity. |
| Bombs dropped: 4–20 lb. | |

| Lieut. F. A. Dixon. | Four bombs on road S.E. of Cambrai. |
|---|---|
| Sopwith Camel, F. 6138. | Fired 300 rounds into moving traffic on |
| Time: 5:00–5:30 P. M. | the Masnières—Cambrai road, just out- |
| Height: 3000–1000 feet. | side Cambrai and on other roads in this |
| Rounds fired: 300. | vicinity. |
| Bombs dropped: 4–20 lb. | |

| Lieut. G. A. Vaughn. | Four bombs on 57b. H. 19–20.  Fired |
|---|---|
| Sopwith Camel, H. 828. | 200 rounds at Cambrai-Rumilly road, |
| Time: 4:55–5:00 P. M. | at a lorry from 500 feet at 5:00 P. M.; |
| Height: 2500–900 feet. | also fired into village (Faubourg de |
| Rounds fired: 200. | Paris), filled with troops. |
| Bombs dropped: 4–20 lb. | |

| Lieut. H. Burdick. | Four bombs on 57b.H.19–20, from |
|---|---|
| Sopwith Camel, F. 2141. | 2500 feet at 4:55 P. M.   Fired 100 |
| Time: 4:55–5:00 P. M. | rounds into Wambaix station and |
| Height: 2500–900 feet. | into a train in station facing E. from |
| Rounds fired: 100. | 2000–900 feet, at 5:00 P. M. |
| Bombs dropped: 4–20 lb. | |

## 15

| 17th Squadron, U.S.A. | No. 6a–29–s. |
|---|---|
| No. and type of machines: | Date: September 29, 1918. |
| Sopwith Camels, C. 8352, | Locality: Cambrai. |
| C. 8337, C. 3351, F. 2142, | |

F. 6211, H. 7272, F. 5993,
F. 2146, H. 7281, F. 6024,
D. 3396, H. 828, F. 2141,
F. 6249.

Lieut. W. W. Goodnow.
Sopwith Camel, C. 8352.
Time: 6:40–7:15 A. M.
Height: 3000 feet.
Rounds fired: nil.
Bombs dropped: 4–20 lb.

Four bombs on Awoingt, 57b.B.26.
Fire in Cambrai, by island in canal,
at 6:40 A. M.

Lieut. J. A. Myers.
Sopwith Camel, C. 8337.
Time: 7:15 A. M.
Height: 3000 feet.
Rounds fired: 50.
Bombs dropped: 4–20 lb.

Four bombs on Awoingt, 57b. B. 26.
Fifty rounds on Cambrai, at 7:15 A. M.

Lieut. J. F. Donoho.
Sopwith Camel, C. 3351.
Time: 7:15 A. M.
Height: 3000 feet.
Rounds fired: nil.
Bombs dropped: 4–20 lb.

Four bombs on Awoingt, 57b. B. 26.

Lieut. C. W. France.
Sopwith Camel, F. 2142.
Time: 6:40–7:15 A. M.
Height: 3000 feet.
Rounds fired: nil.
Bombs dropped: 4–20 lb.

"          "          "

Lieut. F. M. Showalter.
Sopwith Camel, F. 6211.
Time: 6:40–7:15 A. M.
Height: 3000 feet.
Rounds fired: 100.
Bombs dropped: 4–20 lb.

Four bombs on 57b.A.21. Fired 100
rounds at Cambrai, at 7:15 A. M. from
about 3000 feet. Saw fire at Bantigny.
Two large explosions in N.W. part of
Cambrai, at 8:00 A. M.

Lieut. L. J. Desson. Four bombs on 3 four-horse transport
Sopwith Camel, H. 7272. going west, from 3000 feet, at 7:00 A. M.
Time: 6:40–7:15 A. M. Fired 150 rounds at train going south
Height: 3000 feet. into Cambrai, at 7:25 A. M. Seven
Rounds fired: 150. Fokkers over Cambrai at 7:55 A. M.—
Bombs dropped: 4–20 lb. too high for us to attack.

Lieut. J. F. Campbell. Dropped four bombs at 57a.T.23, on
Sopwith Camel, F. 2146. road and R.R., at 7:10 A. M., from 3000
Time: 7:15–8:00 A. M. feet. Large fire in western part of
Height: 3000 feet. Cambrai. Fired 500 rounds on road
Rounds fired: 500. leading east out of Cambrai.
Bombs dropped: 4–20 lb.

Lieut. H. P. Alderman.                 "             "             "
Sopwith Camel, H. 7281.
Time: 6:40–7:15 A. M.
Height: 3000 feet.
Rounds fired: 500.
Bombs dropped: 4–20 lb.

Lieut. M. C. Giesecke.                 "             "             "
Sopwith Camel, D. 3396.
Time: 7:15 A. M.
Height: 3000 feet.
Rounds fired: 100.
Bombs dropped: 4–20 lb.

## 16

17th Squadron, U.S.A. No. 7a-29-s.
No. and type of machines: Date: September 29, 1918.
Sopwith Camels, C. 8352, Locality: Honnecourt, Bantou-
F. 6211, C. 8337, F. 5993, zelle, and Vendhuille.
F. 2164, H. 7281, F. 6024,
D. 3396, F. 2164, F. 2141,
F. 6138, F. 6249.

Lieut. W. W. Goodnow. Dropped four bombs on Honnecourt
Sopwith Camel, C. 8352. (57b.S.7b). Fired 300 rounds at same
Time: 1:30 P. M. town and at Bantouzelle and Vend-
Height: 3500 feet. huille. Cambrai on fire.
Rounds fired: 300.
Bombs dropped: 4–20 lb.

Lieut. F. M. Showalter.
Sopwith Camel, F. 6211.
Time: 1:30 P. M.
Height: 3500 feet.
Rounds fired: 500.
Bombs dropped: 4–20 lb.

Dropped four bombs on Honnecourt (57b.S.7b). Fired 300 rounds at same town and at Bantouzelle and Vendhuille. Cambrai on fire.

Lieut. J. A. Myers.
Sopwith Camel, C. 8337.
Time: 1:30 P. M.
Height: 3500 feet.
Rounds fired: 500.
Bombs dropped: 4–20 lb.

"            "            "

Lieut. J. F. Campbell.
Sopwith Camel, F. 2146.
Time: 1:30 P. M.
Height: 3500 feet.
Rounds fired: 400.
Bombs dropped: 4–20 lb.

"            "            "

Lieut. M. C. Giesecke.
Sopwith Camel, D. 3396.
Time: 1:30 P. M.
Height: 2000 feet.
Rounds fired: 100.
Bombs dropped: 4–20 lb.

Dropped four bombs, at 1:30 P. M., from 2000 feet on Honnecourt. Fired 100 rounds into villages (Bantouzelle and Vendhuille). Heavy M.G. fire from ground. A Camel "N" of 148th Sqdn. seen on back at 57c.J.26c or 25d. A Camel marked "E" on ground on back, on Arras—Doullens road, at 51c.R. Fire in Cambrai, at 57b.A.17d—in a factory. Visibility, nil. Troop movement, nil.

Lieut. A. J. Schneider.
Sopwith Camel, F. 6024.
Time: 1:35 P. M.
Height: 2000 feet.
Rounds fired: 400.
Bombs dropped: 4–20 lb.

400 rounds on bridges and on Vendhuille at working parties and M.G. companies, at 1:35 P. M., from 2000 feet. Dropped four bombs from 2000 feet on Honnecourt.

Lieut. W. T. Clements.
Sopwith Camel, F. 5993.
Time: 1:35 P. M.
Height: 2000 feet.
Rounds fired: 300.

Dropped four bombs on Bantouzelle, at 1:35 P. M., from 2000 feet. Fired 300 rounds on roads leading out of Bantouzelle and on three motor transports, in same place, from 1800 feet.

Bombs dropped: 4–20 lb. One enemy balloon, 2500 feet, four miles N.E. of Bantouzelle.

Lieut. E. D. White.         "        "        "
Sopwith Camel, F. 6194.
Time: 1:35 P. M.
Height: 2000 feet.
Rounds fired: 250.
Bombs dropped: 4–20 lb.

Lieut. H. P. Alderman.       "        "        "
Sopwith Camel, H. 7281. Many fires in Cambrai.
Time: 1:35 P. M.
Height: 2000 feet.
Rounds fired: 700.
Bombs dropped: 4–20 lb.

Lieut. G. A. Vaughn. Dropped four bombs, at 1:35 P. M.,
Sopwith Camel, H. 828. on canal, just north of Honnecourt
Time: 1:35 P. M. (57.b.S7b). Fired 100 rounds at a
Height: 2000 feet. balloon which was pulled down.
Rounds fired: 300.
Bombs dropped: 4–20 lb.

Lieut. F. A. Dixon.        "        "        "
Sopwith Camel, F. 6138.
Time: 1:35 P. M.
Height: 2000 feet.
Rounds fired: 200.
Bombs dropped: 4–20 lb.

Lieut. H. Burdick. Dropped four bombs, at 1:35 P. M.,
Sopwith Camel, F. 2141. on canal, just north of Honnecourt
Time: 1:35 P. M. (57.b.S7b). Fired 100 rounds at a
Height: 2000 feet. balloon which was pulled down.
Rounds fired: 200.
Bombs dropped: 4–20 lb.

## 17

17th Squadron, U.S.A.            No. 8a-1-0.
No. and types of machines:      Date: October 1, 1918.

Sopwith Camels, C. 8352,            Locality: Awoingt.
C. 8337, C. 3351, F. 2142,
F. 6211, F. 5993, F. 2146,
H. 7281, F. 6024, H. 828,
F. 5967, F. 2141, F. 6249,
F. 6138, F. 2164.

Lieut. G. A. Vaughn.     Dropped four bombs on Awoingt; burst
Sopwith Camel, H. 828.  observed in town.
Time: 10:40 A. M.
Height: 3000 feet.
Rounds fired: nil.
Bombs dropped: 4–20 lb.

Lieut. G. D. Wicks.       "        "       "
Sopwith Camel, F. 5967.
Time: 10:40 A. M.
Height: 3000 feet.
Rounds fired: nil.
Bombs dropped: 4–20 lb.

Lieut. H. Burdick.        "        "       "
Sopwith Camel, F. 2141.
Time: 10:40 A. M.
Height: 3000 feet.
Rounds fired: nil.
Bombs dropped: 4–20 lb.

Lieut. E. D. White.      Dropped four bombs on Awoingt; burst
Sopwith Camel, F. 6249.  observed in town.
Time: 10:40 A. M.
Height: 3000 feet.
Rounds fired: nil.
Bombs dropped: 4–20 lb.

Lieut. F. A. Dixon.       "        "       "
Sopwith Camel, F. 6138.
Time: 10:40 A. M.
Height: 3000 feet.
Rounds fired: nil.
Bombs dropped: 4–20 lb.

Lieut. W. W. Goodnow. Dropped four bombs on Awoingt,
Sopwith Camel, C. 8352. about 10:40 A. M., from 3000 feet.
Time: 10:40 A. M. Large explosion observed.
Height: 3000 feet.
Rounds fired: nil.
Bombs dropped: 4–20 lb.


Lieut. J. A. Myers.                    "              "              "
Sopwith Camel, C. 8337.
Time: 10:40 A. M.
Height: 3000 feet.
Rounds fired: nil.
Bombs dropped: 4–20 lb.

Lieut. C. W. France. Dropped four bombs on Awoingt,
Sopwith Camel, F. 2142. about 10:40 A. M. from 3000 feet.
Time: 10:40 A. M. Also observed explosions in Awoingt.
Height: 3000 feet.
Rounds fired: nil.
Bombs dropped: 4–20 lb.


Lieut. F. M. Showalter.                "              "              "
Sopwith Camel, F. 6211.
Time: 10:40 A. M.
Height: 3000 feet.
Rounds fired: nil.
Bombs dropped: 4–20 lb.


Lieut. W. T. Clements. Dropped four bombs on Awoingt, at
Sopwith Camel, F. 5993. 10:40 A. M., from 3000 feet.
Time: 10:40 A. M.
Height: 3000 feet.
Rounds fired: nil.
Bombs dropped: 4–20 lb.


Lieut. J. F. Campbell.                 "              "              "
Sopwith Camel, F. 2146.
Time: 10:40 A. M.
Height: 3000 feet.
Rounds fired: nil.
Bombs dropped: 4–20 lb.

Lieut. H. P. Alderman.       "        "        "
Sopwith Camel, H. 7281.
Time: 10:40 A. M.
Height: 3000 feet.
Rounds fired: nil.
Bombs dropped: 4–20 lb.

Lieut. A. J. Schneider.    Dropped four bombs on Awoingt, at
Sopwith Camel, F. 6024.   10:40 A. M., from 3000 feet.
Time: 10:40 A. M.
Height: 3000 feet.
Rounds fired: nil.
Bombs dropped: 4–20 lb.

Lieut. M. C. Giesecke.       "        "        "
Sopwith Camel, F. 6124.
Time: 10:40 A. M.
Height: 3000 feet.
Rounds fired: nil.
Bombs dropped: 4–20 lb.

## 18

17th Squadron, U.S.A.       No. 9a-1-0.
No. and type of machines:   Date: October 1, 1918.
Sopwith Camels, H. 828,    Locality: Awoingt.
F. 6138, F. 6249, F. 5993,
F. 2146, D. 3396, F. 6024,
C. 3852, C. 3351, F. 2142.

Lieut. W. T. Clements.   Dropped four bombs on Awoingt.
Sopwith Camel, F. 5993.
Time: 5:40 P. M.
Height: 3000 feet.
Rounds fired: nil.
Bombs dropped: 4–20 lb.

Lieut. A. J. Schneider.      "        "        "
Sopwith Camel, F. 6024.

Lieut. G. A. Vaughn.        "        "        "
Sopwith Camel, H. 828.

Lieut. W. W. Goodnow.                     "             "             "
Sopwith Camel, C. 8252.

Lieut. C. W. France.          Dropped four bombs on Awoingt.
Sopwith Camel, F. 2142.

Lieut. J. F. Campbell.                    "             "             "
Sopwith Camel, F. 2146.

Lieut. J. P. Alderman.                    "             "             "
Sopwith Camel, D. 3396.

Lieut. J. F. Donoho.                      "             "             "
Sopwith Camel, C. 3351.

Lieut. E. D. White.                       "             "             "
Sopwith Camel, F. 2649.

Lieut. F. M. Showalter.                   "             "             "
Sopwith Camel, C. 8337.

Lieut. F. A. Dixon.                       "             "             "
Sopwith Camel, F. 6138.

## 19

17th Squadron, U.S.A.              No. 10a-2-0.
No. and type of machines:         Date: October 2, 1918.
Sopwith Camels, H. 828,           Locality: Awoingt.
F. 5967, F. 2141, F. 6138,
F. 6249, C. 8337, F. 5993,
H. 7281, F. 6024, D. 3396,
C. 8352, F. 2142, F. 6211,
C. 3351.

Lieut. G. A. Vaughn.          Dropped four bombs on Awoingt.
Sopwith Camel, H. 828.
Time: 9:10 A. M.
Height: 3500 feet.
Rounds fired: nil.
Bombs dropped: 4-20 lb.

125

Lieut. G. D. Wicks.  Dropped four bombs on Awoingt.
Sopwith Camel, F. 5967.

Lieut. W. W. Goodnow.  "  "  "
Sopwith Camel, C. 8352.

Lieut. J. A. Myers.  "  "  "
Sopwith Camel, C. 8337.

Lieut. F. A. Dixon.  "  "  "
Sopwith Camel, F. 6138.

Lieut. J. F. Campbell.  "  "  "
Sopwith Camel, F. 5993.
Time: 9:10 A. M.
Height: 3000 feet.
Rounds fired: nil.
Bombs dropped: 4–20 lb.

Lieut. C. W. France.  "  "  "
Sopwith Camel, D. 3396.

Lieut. M. C. Giesecke.  "  "  "
Sopwith Camel, F. 2162.

Lieut. F. M. Showalter.  "  "  "
Sopwith Camel, F. 6211.

Lieut. J. F. Donoho.  "  "  "
Sopwith Camel, C. 3351.

Lieut. E. D. White.  "  "  "
Sopwith Camel, F. 6249.

Lieut. A. J. Schneider.  "  "  "
Sopwith Camel, F. 6024.

Lieut. H. P. Alderman.  "  "  "
Sopwith Camel, H. 7281.  Several bursts observed in town.

Lieut. H. Burdick.  "  "  "
Sopwith Camel, F. 2141.

**20**

17th Squadron, U.S.A.  No. 11a–2–0.
No. and type of machines:  Date: October 2, 1918.
Sopwith Camels, F. 5993,  Locality: Awoingt, Wam-
H. 7281, D. 3396, F. 6211,  baix, and 57b.H.7.

F. 2142, C. 3351, C. 8337,
H. 828, F. 5967, F. 6138,
F. 6249, F. 2141.

Lieut. G. A. Vaughn.     Dropped on Awoingt, at 3:30 P. M.
Sopwith Camel, H. 828.
Time: 3:30 P. M.
Height: 3000 feet.
Rounds fired: nil.
Bombs dropped: 4–20 lb.

Lieut. G. D. Wicks.       "      "      "
Sopwith Camel, F. 5967.

Lieut. H. Burdick.        "      "      "
Sopwith Camel, F. 2141.

Lieut. J. F. Campbell.     "      "      "
Sopwith Camel, F. 5993.

Lieut. F. A. Dixon.       Dropped one bomb on Awoingt.
Sopwith Camel, F. 6138.
Bombs dropped: 1–20 lb.

Lieut. J. A. Myers.       Dropped four bombs on Awoingt.
Sopwith Camel, C. 8337.

Lieut. E. D. White.        "      "      "
Sopwith Camel, F. 6249.

Lieut. J. F. Donoho.      "      "      "
Sopwith Camel, C. 3351.

Lieut. H. P. Alderman.'  Dropped four bombs on Awoingt.
Sopwith Camel, H. 7281.  Number of bursts observed. Fire
started.

Lieut. M. C. Giesecke.    "      "      "
Sopwith Camel, D. 3396.

Lieut. C. W. France.     "      "      "
Sopwith Camel, F. 2142.  Fired at 3:40 P. M. 150 rounds on several
lorries on Cambrai—Le Cateau road
from 1500 feet.

Lieut. F. M. Showalter.   Dropped two bombs on Wambaix, and
Sopwith Camel, F. 6211.   two bombs on assembled transport on
                          road between Wambaix and Cambrai,
                          57b.H.7, at 3:40 from 2000 feet.


## 21

17th Squadron, U.S.A.                 No. 12a-2-0.
No. and type of machines:             Date: October 3, 1918.
Sopwith Camels, H. 828,               Locality: Caudry.
F. 2141, F. 5967, F. 6163,
H. 7281, F. 5993, F. 6211,
C. 3351, C. 8337, D. 3396,
F. 2146, F. 6194, C. 8352,
F. 6249.


Lieut. G. A. Vaughn.      Dropped four bombs on Caudry and on
Sopwith Camel, H. 828.    R. R. sidings to the south. Several
Time: 7:35 A. M.          bursts observed in town and near the
Height: 5000 feet.        lines.
Rounds fired: nil.
Bombs dropped: 4–20 lb.


Lieut. H. Burdick.              "          "          "
Sopwith Camel, F. 2141.


Lieut. G. D. Wicks.       Dropped four bombs on Caudry and on
Sopwith Camel, F. 5967.   R. R. sidings to the south. Several
                          bursts observed in town and near the
                          lines.

Lieut. F. A. Dixon.            "          "          "
Sopwith Camel, F. 6163.


Lieut. H. P. Alderman.         "          "          "
Sopwith Camel, H. 7281.


Lieut. C. W. France.           "          "          "
Sopwith Camel, F. 5993.


Lieut. F. M. Showalter.        "          "          "
Sopwith Camel, F. 6211.

Lieut. J. F. Donoho.     "     "     "
Sopwith Camel, C. 3351.

Lieut. M. C. Giesecke.     "     "     "
Sopwith Camel, D. 3396.

Lieut. J. F. Campbell.     "     "     "
Sopwith Camel, F. 2146.

Lieut. H. G. Shoemaker.     "     "     "
Sopwith Camel, F. 6194.

Lieut. W. W. Goodnow.     "     "     "
Sopwith Camel, C. 3852.

Lieut. J. A. Myers.     "     "     "
Sopwith Camel, C. 8337.

Lieut. E. D. White.     Dropped three bombs, as above.   Lost
Sopwith Camel, F. 6429.   formation.   Returned, October 4th, having landed at Borest, near Senlis.

## 22

17th Squadron, U.S.A.     No. 13a-2-0.
No. and type of machines:     Date: October 3, 1918.
Sopwith Camels, H. 828,     Locality: Caudry.
F. 5967, F. 6211, F. 5993,
F. 2146, F. 2141, H. 7281,
F. 6138, F. 6194, C. 3351,
C. 8352, C. 8337, D. 3396.

Lieut. G. A. Vaughn.     Dropped four bombs on R. R. at
Sopwith Camel, H. 828.   Caudry.
Time: 3:10 P. M.
Height: 5000 feet.
Rounds fired: nil.
Bombs dropped: 4–20 lb.

Lieut. G. D. Wicks.     "     "     "
Sopwith Camel, F. 5967.

Lieut. F. M. Showalter.     "     "     "
Sopwith Camel, F. 6211.   A.A. battery working at 57b.I.29.c.90.
Another at 57b.I.32.c.

| | |
|---|---|
| Lieut. C. W. France. | Dropped four bombs at Caudry. Several bursts observed on the R. R. track just outside the station. |
| Sopwith Camel, F. 5993. | |
| | |
| Lieut. J. F. Campbell. | " " " |
| Sopwith Camel, F. 2146. | Burst observed at 57b.I.35.a.37. |
| | |
| Lieut. H. Burdick. | Dropped four bombs on R. R. at Caudry. |
| Sopwith Camel, F. 2141. | |
| | |
| Lieut. H. P. Alderman. | " " " |
| Sopwith Camel, H. 7281. | Fire observed at Rumilly. |
| | |
| Lieut. F. A. Dixon. | " " " |
| Sopwith Camel, F. 6138. | |
| | |
| Lieut. H. G. Shoemaker. | Dropped four bombs on R. R. at Caudry. |
| Sopwith Camel, F. 6194. | Fire observed at Rumilly. |
| | |
| Lieut. J. F. Donoho. | " " " |
| Sopwith Camel, C. 3351. | |
| | |
| Lieut. W. W. Goodnow. | " " " |
| Sopwith Camel, C. 8352. | |
| | |
| Lieut. M. C. Giesecke. | " " " |
| Sopwith Camel, D. 3396. | |
| | |
| Lieut. J. A. Myers. | " " " |
| Sopwith Camel, C. 8337. | Two motor transports at 57b.O.9. |

23

| | |
|---|---|
| 17th Squadron, U.S.A. | No. 142-4-0. |
| No. and type of machines: | Date: October 4, 1918. |
| Sopwith Camels, H. 828, | Locality: Caudry. |
| F. 6194, F. 5967, F. 6138, | |
| C. 8352, C.'8337, C. 3351, | |
| F. 5993, F. 6211, H. 751, | |
| F. 2146, H. 7281. | |

| | |
|---|---|
| Lieut. G. A. Vaughn. | Dropped four bombs on station and train pulling out going east. Heavy A.A. and machine gun fire from ground. |
| Sopwith Camel, H. 828. | |
| Time: 11:30 A. M. | |
| Height: 4000 feet. | |
| Rounds fired: nil. | |
| Bombs dropped: 4–20 lb. | |

Lieut. G. D. Wicks.           "           "           "
Sopwith Camel, F. 5967.

Lieut. F. A. Dixon.           "           "           "
Sopwith Camel, F. 6138.

Lieut. W. W. Goodnow.         "           "           "
Sopwith Camel, C. 8352.

Lieut. J. A. Myers.          Dropped four bombs on station and
Sopwith Camel, C. 8337.      train pulling out going east. Heavy
                             A.A. and machine gun fire from ground.
Lieut. F. M. Showalter.       "           "           "
Sopwith Camel, F. 6211.

Lieut. C. W. France.          "           "           "
Sopwith Camel, F. 2142.

Lieut. L. J. Desson.          "           "           "
Sopwith Camel, H. 751.

Lieut. J. F. Campbell.        "           "           "     .
Sopwith Camel, F. 2146.

Lieut. H. P. Alderman.        "           "           "
Sopwith Camel, H. 7281.

Lieut. J. F. Donoho.         Forced landing at Villeret.
Sopwith Camel, C. 3351.

## 24

17th Squadron, U.S.A.              No. 14a–2–0.
No. and type of machines:         Date: October 4, 1918.
Sopwith Camels, H. 828,           Locality: Awoingt.
F. 2164, F. 2141, F. 6194,
F. 6138, C. 8352, F. 2142,
F. 6211, C. 8337, H. 751.

Lieut. G. A. Vaughn.         Dropped four bombs on Awoingt.
Sopwith Camel, H. 828.       Saw several burst in the town.
Time: 5:30 P. M.

131

Height: 5000 feet.
Rounds fired: nil.
Bombs dropped: 4–20 lb.

| | |
|---|---|
| Lieut. G. D. Wicks.<br>Sopwith Camel, F. 2164. | Dropped four bombs on Awoingt. Saw several burst in the town. |
| Lieut. H. Burdick.<br>Sopwith Camel, F. 2141. | "          "          " |
| Lieut. H. G. Shoemaker.<br>Sopwith Camel, F. 6194. | "          "          " |
| Lieut. F. A. Dixon.<br>Sopwith Camel, F. 6138. | "          "          " |
| Lieut. W. W. Goodnow.<br>Sopwith Camel, C. 8352. | "          "          " |
| Lieut. C. W. France.<br>Sopwith Camel, F. 2142. | "          "          " |
| Lieut. F. M. Showalter.<br>Sopwith Camel, F. 6211. | "          "          " |
| Lieut. J. A. Myers.<br>Sopwith Camel, C. 8337. | "          "          " |
| Lieut. L. J. Desson.<br>Sopwith Camel, H. 751. | "          "          " |

## 25

17th Squadron, U.S.A.
No. and type of machines:
Sopwith Camels, C. 8352,
F. 6211, F. 6024, H. 828,
C. 8337, F. 2142, H. 751,
F. 2146, H. 7281, D. 3396,
F. 6194, F. 5967, F. 2141,
F. 6249, F. 5993.

No. 15a–2–o.
Date: October 5, 1918.
Locality: Awoingt.

Lieut. W. W. Goodnow.    Dropped four bombs on Awoingt.
Sopwith Camel, C. 8352.

Time: 9:00 A. M.
Height: 5000 feet.
Rounds fired: nil.
Bombs dropped: 4–20 lb.

Lieut. F. M. Showalter.          "          "          "
Sopwith Camel, F. 6211.

Lieut. A. J. Schneider.          "          "          "
Sopwith Camel, F. 6024.

Lieut. G. A. Vaughn.          "          "          "
Sopwith Camel, H. 828.    One direct hit on railway station lines.

Lieut. R. W. Snoke.          "          "          "
Sopwith Camel, C. 8337.

Lieut. C. W. France.          "          "          "
Sopwith Camel, F. 2142.

Lieut. J. A. Myers.          "          "          "
Sopwith Camel, H. 751.

Lieut. H. G. Shoemaker.          "          "          "
Sopwith Camel, F. 6194.

Lieut. G. D. Wicks.          "          "          "
Sopwith Camel, F. 5967.

Lieut. H. Burdick.          "          "          "
Sopwith Camel, F. 2141.

Lieut. E. D. White.          "          "          "
Sopwith Camel, F. 6249.

Lieut. J. F. Campbell.          "          "          "
Sopwith Camel, F. 2146.

Lieut. H. P. Alderman.    Dropped four bombs on Awoingt.
Sopwith Camel, F. 2146.

Lieut. M. C. Giesecke.          "          "          "
Sopwith Camel, D. 3396.

Lieut. H. C. Knotts.          "          "          "
Sopwith Camel, F. 5993.  Three hits in village, one on the largest

Time: 9:00 A. M.
Height: 1000 feet.
Rounds fired: nil.
Bombs dropped: 4–20 lb.

building of town, and one on what
seemed sheds near railway station.

## 26

17th Squadron, U.S.A.
No. and type of machines:
Sopwith Camels, F. 2146,
F. 6024, H. 7281, D. 3396,
F. 5993, H. 828, F. 6249
(F. 6194 and F. 5967 missing).

No. 16a–2–0.
Date: October 6, 1918.
Locality: Wambaix and
Esnes.

Lieut. J. F. Campbell.
Sopwith Camel, F. 2146.
Time: 4:35 P. M.
Height: 5000 feet.
Rounds fired: nil.
Bombs dropped: 4–20 lb.

Dropped four bombs on Wambaix.

Lieut. A. J. Schneider.
Sopwith Camel, F. 6024.

" " "

Lieut. H. P. Alderman.
Sopwith Camel, F. 2146.

" " "

Lieut. M. C. Giesecke.
Sopwith Camel, D. 3396.

" " "

Lieut. H. C. Knotts.
Sopwith Camel, F. 5993.

" " "
Saw at least six direct hits on east side
of Wambaix.

Lieut. G. A. Vaughn.
Sopwith Camel, H. 828.
Time: 4:35 P. M.
Height: 4000 feet.
Rounds fired: nil.
Bombs dropped: 4–20 lb.

Four bombs on Esnes. Direct hit seen
on a dump, just west of town (57b.-
E.33.d.), which exploded and was
seen to burn until patrol left, at about
5:10 P.M. Two other fires started. New
fires burning in Cambrai.

Lieut. F. A. Dixon.
Sopwith Camel, F. 6138.

" " "

Lieut. E. D. White.
Sopwith Camel, F. 6249.

" " "
One shell seen to burst on R.R., at
57.C.25, at 4:50 P. M.

Lieut. H. G. Shoemaker.
Sopwith Camel, F. 6194.

Lieut. G. D. Wicks.
Sopwith Camel, F. 5967.

Missing. Collision in air.

## 27

17th Squadron, U.S.A.
No. and type of machines:
Sopwith Camels, H. 828,
F. 2141, F. 6138, F. 6249,
C. 8337, C. 8352, F. 2142,
F. 6211, F. 751, F. 2146,
F. 5993, H. 7281, D. 3396,
F. 6024.

No. 17a–7–o.
Date: October 7, 1918.
Locality: Awoingt and
Cauroir.

Lieut. G. A. Vaughn.
Sopwith Camel, H. 828.
Time: 10:45 A. M.
Height: 5000 feet.
Rounds fired: nil.
Bombs dropped: 4–20 lb.

Dropped four bombs on Awoingt.
Numerous hits in town.

Lieut. H. Burdick.
Sopwith Camel, F. 2141.

Dropped four bombs on Awoingt.

Lieut. E. D. White.
Sopwith Camel, F. 6249.

"          "          "

Lieut. L. J. Desson.
Sopwith Camel, H. 751.

"          "          "

Lieut. J. F. Campbell.
Sopwith Camel, F. 2146.

"          "          "

Lieut. H. C. Knotts.
Sopwith Camel, F. 5993.

"          "          "

Lieut H. P. Alderman.
Sopwith Camel, H. 7281.

"          "          "
Fire started by direct hit on large
building.

Lieut. M. C. Giesecke.
Sopwith Camel, D. 3396.

Dropped four bombs as above.

Lieut. J. F. Donoho.              "           "           "
Sopwith Camel, F. 6024.

Lieut. F. A. Dixon.               "           "           "
Sopwith Camel, F. 6138.

Lieut. R. W. Snoke.    Dropped three bombs on Cauroir at
Sopwith Camel, C. 8337.  10:45 A. M., from 5000 feet. Dropped
one bomb on Awoingt at 10:55 A. M.,
from 5000 feet.

Lieut. J. A. Myers.              "           "           "
Sopwith Camel, C. 8352.

Lieut. C. W. France.            "           "           "
Sopwith Camel, F. 2142.

Lieut. F. M. Showalter.      "           "           "
Sopwith Camel, F. 6211.

## 28

17th Squadron, U.S.A.          No. 18-8-0.
No. and type of machines:      Date: October 8, 1918.
Sopwith Camels, F. 5993,      Locality: East of Cambrai.
H. 7281, D. 3328, H. 828,
F. 2141, H. 751, F. 6138,
F. 6249, F. 2164. C. 3351.

Lieut. H. P. Alderman.    Four bombs on transport going into
Sopwith Camel, H. 7281.  Villers-en-Cauchies also on town. Fired
Time: 12:15 P. M.         250 rounds on road, between Cam-
Height: 1500 feet.         brai and Iwuy, at 12:30–12:45 P. M.,
Rounds fired: 550.         from 150 feet. Fired 300 rounds, from
Bombs dropped: 4–20 lb.  1000 feet, on transport going into town
from Cambrai.

Lieut G. A. Vaughn.      Four bombs on four lorries on road be-
Sopwith Camel, H. 828.   tween Cagnoncles and Naves. Three
Time: 12:15 P. M.         lorries disappeared. Fired on two
Height: 900–1000 feet.    transports, or guns with canvas covers,
Rounds fired: 500.         on road between Cambrai and Naves.
Bombs dropped: 4–20 lb.  One horse was seen to fall in road. In-
fantry, nationality unknown (observed
from 1000 feet) in sunken road running
E. and W., at 57b.B.17, at which I
did not shoot, because they did not fire.

Lieut. H. Burdick.    "   "   "
Sopwith Camel, F. 2141.
Time: 12:15 P. M.
Height: 1500 feet.
Rounds fired: 700.
Bombs dropped: 4–20 lb.

Lieut. F. A. Dixon.    "   "   "
Sopwith Camel, F. 6138.

Lieut. L. J. Desson. Bombs dropped on same target as
Sopwith Camel, H. 751. Lieut. Vaughn. Fired on scattered lorries and infantry marching south between Estourmel and Cattenières. One
Time: 12:15 P. M.
Height: 1500 feet.
Rounds fired: 200. horse transport seen running away.
Bombs dropped: 4–20 lb. Fired 200 rounds from 1000 feet on sunken road, at 57b.H.11.a.22.

Lieut. E. D. White. Four bombs dropped and 300 rounds
Sopwith Camel, F. 6249. fired on same target as Lieut. Vaughn.

Lieut. M. C. Giesecke. Four bombs dropped on Awoingt. 150
Sopwith Camel, F. 2164. rounds fired at factory, 57b.C.25.c
Time: 12:30 P. M. fired from 1000 feet.
Height: 1500 feet.
Rounds fired: 150.
Bombs dropped: 4–20 lb.

Lieut. H. C. Knotts. At 57b.B.19.b.55, direct hit with two
Sopwith Camel, D. 3328. bombs on R.R., from 2000 feet. Small
Time: 12:00–12:40 P. M. motor-driven car on R.R. ran into
Height: 2000–200 feet. break and turned on its side, it
Rounds fired: 600. was full of men who scattered when I
Bombs dropped: 4–20 lb. fired 100 rounds from 1000 feet. Two bombs dropped on Awoingt at 12:40 P. M., from 1500 feet. One hit started fire. 200 rounds fired at a gun being pulled by four horses. Ammunition ran out.

Lieut. J. F. Campbell. Four bombs dropped on two lorries
Sopwith Camel, F. 5993. on road, at 51a.T.15, at 12:40 P. M.
Time: 12:15-12:40 P. M. 300 rounds fired on them before drop-
Height: 2000 feet. ping bombs. 200 rounds fired at lorry
Rounds fired: 500. at 51a.T.10.
Bombs dropped: 4–20 lb.

Lieut J. F. Donoho. Four bombs dropped on R.R., at
Sopwith Camel, C. 3351. 51b.B.2, at 12:00, from 2000 feet.
Time: 12:00–12:30 P. M. 200 rounds fired on two lorries, at
Height: 1000 feet. 57b.C.11. Lorries disappeared when
Rounds fired: 400. I zoomed and turned back. Fired
Bombs dropped: 4–20 lb. 200 into trenches, at 57b.B.11.

**29**

17th Squadron, U.S.A. No. 19-8-0.
No. and type of machines: Date: October 8, 1918.
Sopwith Camels, C. 8352,
C. 3351, F. 6211, F. 2007,
F. 2146, F. 7281, F. 5993,
D. 3396, F. 6024, F. 6138.

Lieut. F. M. Showalter. Four bombs dropped on town, from
Sopwith Camel, F. 6211. 1500 feet. Fired 700 rounds on trans-
Time: 4:45 P. M. port and troops, at 57b.B.17, in
Height: 1500–1000 feet. sunken road, at 5:00 P. M., from 1000
Rounds fired: 700. feet. Other roads full of transport.
Bombs dropped: 4–20 lb.

Lieut. W. W. Goodnow. Four bombs dropped on transport be-
Sopwith Camel, C. 8352. tween Cambrai and Beauvois. Fired
Time: 4:40 P. M. 350 rounds at same time from 2000 feet.
Height 3000–2000 feet. Explosion seen at Sucrerie, just south
Rounds fired: 350. of Cattenières, at 4:50 P. M.
Bombs dropped: 4–20 lb.

Lieut. M. C. Giesecke. One bomb dropped on troops along
Sopwith Camel, D. 3396. side R.R., at 57b.B.20. One bomb on
Time: 4:30–4:35 P. M. Cambrai-Saulzoir road, on troops, from
Height: 900 feet. 900 feet, at 4:35 P. M. Two bombs on
Rounds fired: 500. Cambrai—St. Vaast road at 57b.B.6, on
Bombs dropped: 4–20 lb. troops. Fired 200 rounds at horse
transport going from Cambrai to
Naves, from 500 feet. 300 more rounds
on group of troops, at 57b.B.18, from
400 feet at 4:50 P. M.

**Lieut. J. F. Campbell.**
Sopwith Camel, F. 2146.

No bombs dropped. Returned early with engine trouble.

**Lieut. J. A. Myers.**
Sopwith Camel, F. 2007.
Time: 4:30–5:00 P. M.
Height: 2000 feet.
Rounds fired: 200.
Bombs dropped: nil.

Fired 200 rounds, from 2000 feet, at various fleeting targets—transport on Cambrai—Naves road, troops on railway between Cambrai and Caudry.

**Lieut. C. W. France.**
Sopwith Camel, F. 6024.
Time: 4:35–5:05 P. M.
Height: 1500–900 feet.
Rounds fired: 350.
Bombs dropped: 4–20 lb.

Two bombs dropped on sunken road (57b.B.17–18), from 1500 feet at 4:35 P. M. Fired 100 rounds on same target. Fired 150 rounds at transport going east on Cambrai—Naves road, from 900 feet, at 5:00 P. M. Fired 100 rounds at troops on crossroads of Cambrai—Valenciennes and Cambrai—Le Cateau roads. Two bombs on transport on Cambrai—Naves road.

**Lieut. H. P. Alderman.**
Sopwith Camel, H. 7281.
Time: 4:40–5:00 P. M.
Height: 150 feet.
Rounds fired: 700.
Bombs dropped: 4–20 lb.

Four bombs dropped on 57b.B.15a. 22. Fired 700 rounds on transport moving east of Cambrai—Saulzoir road, also on road from Villers-en-Cauchies to St. Aubert. Observed much confusion in these small detachments when they were fired upon.

**Lieut. H. C. Knotts,**
Sopwith Camel, F. 5993.
Time: 4:30 P. M.
Height: 2000–50 feet.
Rounds fired: 500.
Bombs dropped: 4–20 lb.

Four bombs dropped from 2000 feet on troops; followed them down firing 100 rounds; saw many fall; went down to fifty feet. Fired 100 rounds on battery and lorry with eight men, from 50 feet, at 51a.U.13.c.55. Results not observed. 300 rounds fired on two vehicles, at 51a.T.22.c. 05; driver ran ahead and fell at 51a.T.18.d; horses seen to fall also. Severe machine gun fire from 51a.U.13.d.08.

**Lieut. R. W. Snoke.**
Sopwith Camel, F. 6138.
Time: 4:35 P. M.
Height: 2000 feet.
Rounds fired: 150.
Bombs dropped, 4–20 lb.

Four bombs dropped on troops at 57b.B.27. Saw one burst among troops. Fired 150 rounds at horse transport on main road, at 57b.B.27. Saw horses fall.

Lieut. J. F. Donoho.       Four bombs dropped at 51a.T.20,
Sopwith Camel, C. 3351.    from 2000 feet, at 4:35 P. M., on trans-
Time: 4:35 P. M.           port. Fired 400 rounds from 1000
Height: 2000 feet.         feet at transport along road, same
Rounds fired: 400.         place. Much confusion caused.
Bombs dropped: 4–20 lb.

## 30

17th Squadron, U.S.A.              No. 2-09-0.
No. and type of machines:         Date: October 9, 1918.
Sopwith Camels: F. 2146,
H. 7281, D. 3328, D. 3396,
F. 6024, C. 8352, C. 3351,
F. 6211, F. 2007, F. 6249,
F. 2164, H. 751, F. 6138.

Lieut. F. M. Showalter.    Four bombs dropped on R.R., north
Sopwith Camel, F. 6211.    of Awoingt, from 2000 feet, at 6:40
Time: 6:40 A. M.           A. M.   Bursts seen at edge of railroad.
Height: 2000 feet.
Rounds fired: nil.
Bombs dropped: 4–20 lb.

Lieut. J. F. Donoho.       Four bombs dropped on 51a.U.19.
Sopwith Camel, C. 3351.    No movement on roads.
Time: 6:40 A. M.
Height: 2000 feet.
Rounds fired: nil.
Bombs dropped: 4–20 lb.

Lieut. J. F. Campbell.     Four bombs dropped on 51a.U.19.
Sopwith Camel, F. 2146.    No movement on roads.

Lieut. H. C. Knotts.             "          "          "
Sopwith Camel, D. 3328.

Lieut. H. P. Alderman.           "          "          "
Sopwith Camel, H. 7281.

Lieut. C. W. France.       Four bombs dropped on Cauroir, from
Sopwith Camel, F. 6024.    5000 feet, at 6:40 A. M.

Lieut. W. W. Goodnow.      Four bombs dropped on Awoingt, from
Sopwith Camel, C. 8352.    5000 feet, at 6:30 A. M.
Time: 6:30 A. M.
Height: 5000 feet.
Rounds fired: nil.
Bombs dropped: 4–20 lb.


Lieut. J. A. Myers.          "          "          "
Sopwith Camel, F. 2007.


Lieut. M. C. Giesecke.      Two bombs dropped on Awoingt, from
Sopwith Camel, D. 3396.    5000 feet, at 6:30 A. M. two bombs on
                           Cauroir, from 3000, at 6:35 A. M.


Lieut. F. A. Dixon.         Four bombs dropped on Rieux, from
Sopwith Camel, F. 6138.    5000 feet, at 6:30 A. M.


Lieut. L. J. Desson.         "          "          "
Sopwith Camel, H. 751.


Lieut. H. Burdick.           "          "          "
Sopwith Camel, F. 2164,


Lieut. G. A. Vaughn.        Four bombs dropped on Cauroir, at
Sopwith Camel, F. 6249.    6:30 A. M.

### 31

17th Squadron, U.S.A.       No. 21-9-0.
No. and type of machines:   Date: October 9, 1918.
Sopwith Camels, D. 9423,
F. 2146, H. 7281, C. 3351,
D. 3396.

Major H. L. Fowler.         Four bombs dropped on Rieux R.R.
Sopwith Camel, D. 9423.    sidings, at 51a.O.19, at 1:20 P. M., from
Time: 1:20 P. M.           5000 feet.
Height: 5000 feet.
Rounds fired: nil.
Bombs dropped: 4–20 lb.


Lieut. J. F. Campbell.       "          "          "
Sopwith Camel, F. 2146.

Lieut. H. P. Alderman.　　　"　　　　"　　　　"
Sopwith Camel, H. 7281.

Lieut. J. F. Donoho.　　　One bomb dropped on same target.
Sopwith Camel, C. 3351.

Lieut. M. C. Giesecke.　　One bomb dropped on St. Hilaire.
Sopwith Camel, D. 3396.　Explosion seen at 1:35 P. M., near
　　　　　　　　　　　　Avesnes-lez-Aubert.

Total: 19–20 lb. bombs dropped.

## 32

17th Squadron, U.S.A.　　　　　No 22-14-0.
No. and type of machines:　　　Date: October 14, 1918.
Sopwith Camels, H. 828,　　　　Locality: Bazuel.
H. 830, H. 757, F. 6138,
F. 6249, C. 8352, C. 8337,
C. 3351, F. 2006, F. 2007,
F. 6211, F. 2146, D. 3328,
H. 7281, D. 3396.

Lieut. G. A. Vaughn.　　　Dropped four bombs at 7:10 A. M., on
Sopwith Camel, H. 828.　Bazuel, from 3000 feet. Bursts seen
Time: 7:10 A. M.　　　　　along the road. Very heavy machine
Height: 3000 feet.　　　　gun fire and anti-aircraft fire from
Rounds fired: nil.　　　　ground. Large machine gun nest in
Bombs dropped: 4–20 lb.　Bazuel.　　Visibility bad.　　Balloons
　　　　　　　　　　　　seen at 51.S.19–25.

Lieut. H. Burdick.　　　　"　　　　"　　　　"
Sopwith Camel, H. 830.

Lieut. L. J. Desson.　　　"　　　　"　　　　"
Sopwith Camel, H. 751.

Lieut. F. A. Dixon.　　　　"　　　　"　　　　"
Sopwith Camel, F. 6138.

Lieut. W. R. House.　　　　"　　　　"　　　　"
Sopwith Camel, F. 6249.

Lieut. W. W. Goodnow.　　"　　　　"　　　　"
Sopwith Camel, C. 8352.

Lieut. J. F. Campbell.　　　"　　　　"　　　　"
Sopwith Camel, F. 2146.

Lieut. R. W. Snoke.          "        "        "
Sopwith Camel, C. 8337.

Lieut. J. F. Donoho.      •   "      "      "
Sopwith Camel, C. 3351.

Lieut. H. C. Knotts.       "      "      "
Sopwith Camel, D. 3328.

Lieut. H. P. Alderman.     "      "      "
Sopwith Camel, H. 7281.

Lieut. F. M. Showalter.    "      "      "
Sopwith Camel, F. 6211.

Lieut. M. C. Giesecke.   Three bombs dropped on same target.
Sopwith Camel, D. 3396.

Total: 51–20 lb. bombs dropped.

## 33

17th Squadron, U.S.A.         No. 23-14,-0.
No. and type of machines:    Date: October 14, 1918.
Sopwith Camels, F. 2146,
D. 3328, H. 7281, D. 3396,
F. 5993, C. 8352, C. 8337,
C. 3351, F. 2007, F. 6211,
H. 828, H. 830, H. 751,
F. 6138, F. 6249.

Lieut. J. F. Campbell.    Shot up transport on Verchain road, at
Sopwith Camel, F. 2146.  51a.Q.2.0.  200 rounds fired into the
Time: 1:40 P. M.       villages of Monchaux and Quérenaing.
Height: 2500 feet.
Rounds fired: 500.
Bombs dropped: 4–20 lb.

Lieut. H. C. Knotts.     Not returned; was seen to land and
Sopwith Camel, D. 3328.  get out of his machine, at 51a.P.28.

Lieut. H. P. Alderman.   Fired 150 rounds at transport near
Sopwith Camel, H. 7281.  Vendegies.
Rounds fired: 150.

Lieut. M. C. Giesecke.   Four bombs dropped on troops in
Sopwith Camel, D. 3396.  sunken road at 51a.P.29.  Fired 100
Time: 1:40 P. M.       rounds at transport at 51a.P.24.  Big
Rounds fired: 100.      fire in Solesmes.

| | |
|---|---|
| Lieut. C. W. France. | Four bombs dropped on transport, at |
| Sopwith Camel, F. 5993. | 51a.Q.19.   200 rounds fired at same |
| Rounds fired: 350. | transport.  150 rounds at another target nearby. |
| | |
| Lieut. W. W. Goodnow. | Four bombs dropped on transport just |
| Sopwith Camel, C. 8352. | south of Vendegies.  200 rounds fired |
| Time: 1:30 P. M. | at same transport.   Fired 200 rounds |
| Height: 2500 feet. | at pom-pom battery at Vendegies. |
| Rounds fired: 400. | |
| | |
| Lieut. J. A. Myers. | 100 rounds fired at transport, south of |
| Sopwith Camel, F. 2007. | Vendegies. |
| Rounds fired: 100. | |
| | |
| Lieut. R. W. Snoke. | Four bombs dropped and 100 rounds |
| Sopwith Camel, C. 8337. | fired on transport, at 51a.Q.19. |
| Rounds fired: 100. | |
| | |
| Lieut. J. F. Donoho. | Four bombs dropped on transport, at |
| Sopwith Camel, G. 3351. | 51a.Q.20. |
| | |
| Lieut. F. M. Showalter. | Four bombs dropped and 500 rounds |
| Sopwith Camel, F. 6211. | fired on transport on road leading |
| Rounds fired: 500. | through Villers-Pol. |
| | |
| Lieut. G. A. Vaughn. | Four bombs dropped and 300 rounds |
| Sopwith Camel, H. 828. | fired on transport along road, just east |
| Time: 2:10 P. M. | of Verchain. |
| Rounds fired: 300. | |
| | |
| Lieut. W. R. House. | "          "          " |
| Sopwith Camel, F. 6249. | |
| Rounds fired: 150. | |
| | |
| Lieut. L. J. Desson. | Four bombs dropped and 100 rounds |
| Sopwith Camel, H. 751. | fired on transport along road near Ver- |
| Time: 2:10 P. M. | chain. |
| Height: 2500 feet. | |
| Rounds fired: 100. | |
| Bombs dropped: 4–20 lb. | |
| | |
| Lieut. F. A. Dixon. | Four bombs dropped and 750 rounds |
| Sopwith Camel, F. 6138. | fired on transport, at 51a.Q.19. |
| Rounds fired: 750. | |
| | |
| Lieut. H. Burdick. | Three bombs dropped and 150 rounds |
| Sopwith Camel, H. 830. | fired on transport just east of Verchain. |

Time: 1:40 P. M.
Height: 1500 feet.
Rounds fired: 750.
Bombs dropped: 3–20 lb.

Used remaining ammunition shooting down and firing at Fokker on ground, killing pilot.

Total: 55–20 lb. bombs dropped; 4300 rounds fired.

## 34

17th Squadron, U.S.A.
No. and type of machines:
Sopwith Camels, F. 5993,
F. 6024, H. 7281.

No. 24-24-0.
Date: October 24, 1918.

Lieut. W. T. Clements.
Sopwith Camel, F. 5993.
Time: 2:05 P. M.
Height: 300 feet.
Rounds fired: nil.
Bombs dropped: 4–20 lb.

Four bombs dropped on Landrecies-Maroilles road, at 51.H.20. Visibility poor. Heavy clouds. No movements on roads through Mormal Forest.

Lieut. A. J. Schneider.
Sopwith Camel, F. 6024.
Time: 2:05 P. M.
Height: 300 feet.
Rounds fired: nil.
Bombs dropped: 4–20 lb.

"         "         "

Lieut. H. P. Alderman.
Sopwith Camel, H. 7281.
Time: 2:05 P. M.
Height: 300 feet.
Rounds fired: nil.
Bombs dropped: 4–20 lb.

"         "         "

Total: 12–20 lb. bombs dropped.

CHAPTER 7

# Statistics

PART 1

Record of the 17th Squadron During Active Operations for the Period July 15—October 28, 1918

*1.* Number of enemy aircraft destroyed and confirmed 53

*2.* Number of enemy aircraft driven down out of control 11

*3.* Total number of enemy aircraft destroyed and driven down 64

*4.* Number of days, on which offensive patrols were sent over the lines 51

*5.* Number of machines sent on offensive patrol 936

*6.* Number of hours flown on offensive patrol 1893

*7.* Number of enemy aircraft destroyed or driven down out of control for each flying day 1.25½

*8.* Number of days of low bombing raids and machine gun attacks on enemy transport and infantry 16

*9.* Number of low bombing raids and machine gun attacks sent out 36

*10.* Number of hours flown on low bombing raids and attacks on enemy transport and infantry 462

*11.* Number of bombs dropped 1164

*12.* Total weight of bombs dropped (in pounds) 23780

*13.* Number of machines sent over lines on low bombing raids and attacks on enemy transport and infantry 314

*14.* Number of rounds fired on enemy transport and infantry 31806

*15.* Number of line patrols carried out 15

*16.* Number of days on which line patrols were carried out 8

17. Number of hours of line patrol 248
18. Number of machines sent out on line patrol 183
19. Number of decorations (D.F.C.) awarded pilots by British 5
20. Number of American decorations (D.S.C.) 1
21. Number of mentions in R.A.F. *Communiqués* 35
22. Number of days of active service 105
23. Number of days of bad weather during active service 20
24. Number of days of moving or refitting 10
25. Average number of machines serviceable 16

## PART 2

### Victories and Losses Tabulated

July, 1918

Enemy Aeroplanes destroyed:

| | |
|---|---:|
| July 20 | 1 |
| Total | 1 |

Losses:

| | |
|---|---:|
| July 20 (Missing from offensive patrol) 1st Lieut. | 1 |
| Total | 1 |

August, 1918

Enemy Aeroplanes destroyed:

| | |
|---|---:|
| August 1 | 1 |
| August 3 | 2 |
| August 7 | 3 |
| August 13 | 14[1] |
| August 14 | 2 |
| August 21 | 1 |
| August 22 | 1 |
| August 25 | 1 |
| August 26 | 5 |
| Total | 30 |

Enemy Balloons destroyed:

| | |
|---|---:|
| August 21 | 1 |
| August 22 | 1 |
| August 24 | 1 |
| Total | 3 |

---

1. Eight confirmed by R.A.F. *Communiqué* No. 20, dated August 13. Fourteen confirmed by prisoner of war, as stated in R.A.F. Summary of Intelligence, dated October 20.

Enemy Aeroplanes driven down out of control:

| | |
|---|---|
| August 1 | 1 |
| August 8 | 1 |
| August 9 | 1 |
| August 12 | 1 |
| August 21 | 1 |
| August 22 | 1 |
| August 26 | 1 |
| Total | 7 |

Losses:

| | | |
|---|---|---|
| August 4 (Missing from offensive patrol) | 1st Lieut. | 1 |
| August 12 (Missing from offensive patrol) | 1st Lieut. | 1 |
| August 14 (Missing from offensive patrol) | 1st Lieut. | 1 |
| (Missing from offensive patrol) | 2nd Lieut. | 1 |
| August 23 (Wound. on low bomb. patrol) | 1st Lieut. | 1 |
| (Killed on low bombing patrol) | 1st Lieut. | 1 |
| August 24 (Prisoner of war) | 2nd Lieut. | 1 |
| (Killed on low bombing patrol) | 1st Lieut. | 1 |
| August 26 (Prisoners of war) | 1st Lieut. | 1 |
| (Prisoner of war) | 2nd Lieut. | 1 |
| (Missing from offensive patrol) | 1st Lieut. | 1 |
| (Missing from offensive patrol) | 2nd Lieut. | 2 |
| Total | | 14 |

September, 1918.

Enemy Aeroplanes destroyed:

| | |
|---|---|
| September 13 | 1 |
| September 17 | 1 |
| September 18 | 1 |
| September 22 | 4 |
| September 24 | 5 |
| September 28 | 3 |
| Total | 15 |

Enemy Aeroplanes driven down out of control:

| | |
|---|---|
| September 18 | 1 |
| September 24 | 1 |
| September 27 | 1 |
| Total | 3 |

Enemy Kite Balloons apparently destroyed but not confirmed:

| | |
|---|---|
| September 18 | 1 |
| Total | 1 |

Losses:

September 22 (Pris. of war; afterwards escaped) 1st Lieut.   1
        (Missing from offensive patrol) 2nd Lieut.   1
        Total   2
   October, 1918.

Enemy Aeroplanes destroyed:
   October 2   1
   October 14   2
   October 25   1
       Total   4

Losses:
October 6 (Missing from bombing patrol)   1st Lieut.   1
      (Killed while on bombing patrol) 1st Lieut.   1
October 14 (Prisoner of war)   2nd Lieut.   1
      Total.   3

| | |
|---|---|
| Total aeroplanes destroyed and confirmed | 50 |
| Total balloons destroyed and confirmed | 3 |
| Total enemy aircraft destroyed and confirmed | 53 |
| Total aeroplanes driven down out of control | 10 |
| Total balloons apparently destroyed | 1 |
| Total enemy aircraft destroyed and out of control | 64 |

Total losses:
| | |
|---|---|
| Wounded | 1 |
| Prisoners of war | 6 |
| Missing | 10 |
| Killed | 3 |
| Total | 20 |

PART 3

Record of the 17th Squadron, in the Technical Upkeep and Repair of Sopwith Camel Aeroplanes and Le Rhone Engines, During Active Operations

Number of machines drawn from British 66
Establishment 19
Consumption 47
Average consumption per month $10^{11/13}$
Lost over lines ($40^{2/5}$ %) 19
Returned as time expired ($6^{2/5}$ %) 3
Crashed or shot beyond repair ($53^{1/5}$ %) 25

149

Spare engines received 28

Establishment 9

Consumption 19

Average running time of engines overhauled in Squadron 34 hrs. 57½ min.

Longest run in Squadron before overhaul 86 hrs. 15 min.

Average number of spare engines kept serviceable 5.3

Record for Timing and Maintenance of C. C. Gears:

Average number of rounds fired without shooting propeller 27500

Record of R.A.F. Brigades for September, 1918 22800

# Appendix

## Part 1

Casualties and Changes in Officers of 17th Squadron During Overseas Service

*October 11*, 1917 1st Lieut. David T. Wells attached to Squadron as Supply Officer (Assigned, December 31, 1917.)

*January 8*, 1918 1st Lieut. James G. Bennett assigned as pilot.

*June 4* 1st Lieut. Lorenz K. Ayers assigned as Armament Officer.

*June 20* 1st Lieut. Samuel B. Eckert assigned as Commanding Officer.

*June 21* Assigned: 1st Lieut. Frederick M. Clapp as Adjutant.

1st Lieut. Morton L. Newhall as Flight Commander.

1st Lieut. Lloyd A. Hamilton as Flight Commander.

1st Lieut. Weston W. Goodnow as Flight Commander.

1st Lieuts. Rodney D. Williams, Merton L. Campbell, Henry B. Frost, and William D. Tipton as pilots.

1st Lieut. Henry McC. Bangs relieved from duty as Adjutant.

*June 23* 1st Lieuts. Murray K. Spidle, Laurence Roberts, Floyd M. Showalter, George P. Glenn, Harriss P. Alderman, Lyman E. Case, and 2nd Lieut. Robert M. Todd assigned as pilots.

*June 26* 1st Lieuts. Ralph D. Gracie, Bradley C. Lawton, Ralph W. Snoke, Frank A. Dixon, William J. Armstrong, and Leonard J. Desson assigned as pilots.

*July 1* 1st Lieut. Theose E. Tillinghast and 2nd Lieut. William H. Shearman assigned as pilots. 1st Lieut. Morton L. Newhall relieved from duty and assigned as Commanding Officer to 148th Aero Squadron.

*July 6* 1st Lieut. Jacob J. Ross attached as Medical Officer.

Active Operations

*July 20* 1st Lieut. George P. Glenn "missing" from patrol escorting 211 Squadron, R.A.F., over lines. Dropped from rolls, July 28.

*July 21* 1st Lieut. Albert J. Schneider and 2nd Lieut. George T. Wise assigned as pilots.

*July 26* 1st Lieut. Bradley C. Lawton to No. 13 General Hospital, as result of fall in machine at Adinkerque on July 11. Dropped from rolls July 28.

*July 27* 1st Lieut. Laurence Roberts admitted sick to No. 40 General Hospital, B.E.F., Calais. Dropped from rolls, July 29.

*July 30* 1st Lieut. Leonard J. Desson admitted sick to Queen Alexandra Hospital.

*August 1* 1st Lieuts. Glenn D. Wicks and Jesse F. Campbell assigned as pilots.

*August 4* 1st Lieut. Murray K. Spidle "missing" from O.P. Dropped from rolls, August 5. 1st Lieut. Leonard J. Desson returned to squadron from hospital.

*August 12* 1st Lieut. William J. Armstrong admitted to Queen Alexandra Hospital, wounded in combat. Dropped from rolls, August 14.

*August 12* 2nd Lieut. Harry H. Jackson assigned as pilot. 1st Lieut. Ralph D. Grade "missing" from O.P. Dropped from rolls, August 13.

1st Lieut. Ralph W. Snoke admitted to Queen Alexandra Hospital as result of injuries received in landing on aerodrome.

*August 13* 1st Lieut. Harriss P. Alderman admitted to Queen Alexandra Hospital, wounded in combat.

*August 14* 1st Lieut. Lyman E. Case "missing"; last seen falling from 14000 feet after collision with Fokker shot down by Lieut. Wicks. Dropped from rolls, August 16. 2nd Lieut. William H. Shearman "missing" from O.P. Dropped from rolls, August 16.

*August 14* 1st Lieut. Harriss P. Alderman to duty from hospital.

*August 15* 1st Lieut. Albert F. Everett assigned as pilot. 2nd Lieut. John F. Donoho assigned as pilot.

*August 16* 2nd Lieuts. Howard P. Bittinger, Howard Burdick, and Howard C. Knotts assigned as pilots.

*August 17* 1st Lieut. Ralph W. Snoke to duty from hospital.

*August 23* 1st Lieut. Merton L. Campbell "missing" from low bombing show. Dropped from rolls, August 29.

1st Lieut. Laurence Roberts reassigned as pilot. 1st Lieut. Rodney D. Williams wounded on low bombing show.

Landed at 3 Squadron, R.A.F., and sent to CCS. at Gézaincourt. Dropped from rolls, August 27.

*August 24* 1st Lieut. Lloyd A. Hamilton "missing" from low bombing show.

Last seen spinning to earth after shooting down enemy balloon, east of Bapaume. Dropped from rolls, August 27.

*August 24* 2nd Lieut. George T. Wise "missing" from low bombing show over lines. Dropped from rolls, August 27.

*August 26* 1st Lieuts. William D. Tipton, Henry B. Frost, 2nd Lieuts. Robert M. Todd, Harry H. Jackson, Jr., Howard P. Bittinger, and 1st Lieut. Laurence Roberts "missing" from O.P. Dropped from rolls, Aug. 29.

*August 28* 1st Lieut. James G. Bennett to detached ser- vice, England, for further training in flying.

*August 29* 1st Lieuts. George A. Vaughn, Jr., William T. Clements, Thomas L. Moore, Charles W. France, and Harold G. Shoemaker assigned as pilots.

*August 30* 2nd Lieuts. Gerald P. Thomas and John A. Myers assigned as pilots.

*August 31* 1st Lieut. Harriss P. Alderman admitted to hospital for wounds to heal completely. 2nd Lieut. James A. Ellison assigned as pilot.

*Sept. 2* 1st Lieut. Albert F. Everett admitted sick to 21 CCS. Hospital. Dropped from rolls Sept. 4.

*Sept. 3* 1st Lieut. Martin C Giesecke assigned as pilot.

*Sept. 5* 1st Lieut. Thomas L. Moore transferred to 148th Aero Squadron.

*Sept. 11* 2nd Lieut. Irving P. Corse assigned as pilot.

*Sept. 13* 2nd Lieut. Irving P. Corse admitted sick to No. 18 General Hospital. 1st Lieut. Joseph L. Mulcahy attached to Squadron for 10 days duty as Dental Officer. 1st Lieut. Jacob J. Ross, M.C, to special duty at No. 14 General Hospital.

*Sept. 17* 1st Lieut. William H. Spindle and 2nd Lieut. Edgar G. White assigned as pilots.

*Sept. 22* 1st Lieut. Jacob J. Ross, M.C., to duty from special duty.

1st Lieut. Theose E. Tillinghast and 2nd Lieut. Gerald P. Thomas "missing" from O.P. Dropped from rolls Sept. 24.

*Sept. 24* 1st Lieut. William H. Spindle admitted sick to No. 14

General Hospital. Dropped from rolls Sept. 26.

*Sept. 26* 2nd Lieut. Howard C. Knotts admitted sick to 18 General Hospital.

*Sept. 27* 1st Lieut. Harriss P. Alderman to duty from hospital.

*Oct. 2* 1st Lieut. Joseph L. Mulcahy, dentist, to II Corps.

*Oct. 5* 2nd Lieut. Howard C. Knotts to duty from hospital.

*Oct. 6* 2nd Lieut. William R. House assigned as pilot. 1st Lieuts. Harold G. Shoemaker and Glenn D. Wicks "missing" from O.P. and bombing patrol. Dropped from rolls Oct. 7.

*Oct. 8* 2nd Lieut. Edgar G. White admitted to 21 CCS. Hospital, wounded on O.P. Dropped from rolls Oct. 10.

*Oct. 13* 1st Lieut. Albert F. Everett reassigned as pilot.

*Oct. 15* 2nd Lieut. Howard C Knotts "missing" from offensive and bombing patrol. Dropped from rolls Oct. 18.

*Oct. 16* 1st Lieut. George A. Vaughn, Jr., admitted sick to hospital.

*Oct. 21* 2nd Lieut. James A. Ellison admitted sick to hospital. Dropped from rolls Oct. 23.

*Oct. 22* 1st Lieuts. Cuthbert Tunstall and Ernest S. Mason and 2nd Lieuts. Edward S. Lubbers and William F. Schadt assigned as pilots.

*Oct. 24* 1st Lieut. George A. Vaughn, Jr., from hospital to duty.

*Oct. 26* 1st Lieut. William J. Armstrong reassigned as pilot.

*Oct. 28* 1st Lieut. Albert J. Schneider admitted sick to 20 General Hospital.

*Nov. 1* Squadron assigned to 4th Pursuit Group, II Army, American E.F.

## Part 2

Roster of Enlisted Men Who have Been Members of 17th Squadron Since Its Arrival Overseas[1]

Alexander, 19815, Cpl.
Jasper Allen, 19834, Roy J. Pvt. 1st Cl.
Anthony, 19827, Earl H. Pvt. 1st Cl.
Apel, 19739, Virden J. Pvt. 1st Cl.
Aten, 19790, Merritt C. Pvt. 1st Cl.
Atwood, 19733, Leon Pvt. 1st Cl.

---

1. All enlisted men came Overseas originally with the 17th Squadron unless otherwise designated.

Bailey, 19728, Paul Cpl.

Baker, 19827, Maurice Pvt.

Bardot, 19740, Harry E. Pvt. 1st Cl.

Barr, 19773, Robert J. Sgt. 1st Cl.

Bauer, 19683, Edward C. Sgt. 1st Cl.

Beaudet, 19843, Alfred L. Pvt.

Beebe, 19835, Albert J. Pvt. 1st Cl.

Beebe, 19840, Claude R. Cpl.

Beers, 19876, Lloyd S. Pvt.

Berntsen, 19844, Carl Pvt. 1st Cl.

Bigelow, 1116855, Erwin D. Pvt. Transferred to squadron from II Corps Replacement Battalion, October 6, 1918.

Blunt, 19797, Milton A. Cpl.

Boomer, 19727, Charles E. Cpl.

Booth, 19701, Claud L. Pvt.

Booth, 19741, Clifton W. Pvt.

Bower, 19695, Bishop F. Pvt.

Bowman, 1079338, Augustine C. Pvt. Transferred to squadron from II Corps Replacement Battalion, October 6, 1918.

Brooks, 19827, Bernard R. Chauf.

Brown, 19836, Benjamin A. Cpl.

Brown, 19686, Ned C. Pvt. 1st Cl..

Brown, 19742, Ney S. Chauf.

Buchanan, 19690, Robert B. Cpl.

Buck, 19845, Selby H. Pvt.

Bunyan, 19737, John A. Pvt. 1st CI.

Burns, 19691, Forrest L. Chauf.

Cale, 37474, Jesse C. Pvt. Transferred to squadron from II Corps Replacement Battalion, October 6, 1918.

Casement, 37325, Will B. Pvt. Transferred to squadron from II Corps Replacement Battalion, October 6, 1918.

Chapman, 19743, Garrett B. Pvt.

Cobb, 19744, John L. Pvt.

Conklin, 19745, Orrin Pvt. 1st Cl.

Cooper, 19746, Loran J. Pvt.

Cotner, 19750, Earl R. Pvt. Transferred from squadron to Re-classification Barracks, October 24, 1918.

Covan, 19702, James H. Pvt.

Cox, 1058760, Daniel J. Pvt. Transferred to squadron from II Corps Replacement Battalion, October 6, 1918.

Cox, 19698, Reginald N. Pvt. 1st Cl. Admitted to No. 45 Base Hospital, Toul, November 14, 1918. Dropped from rolls, November 23, 1918.

Cox, 19846, Tom W. Pvt. Admitted to No. 21 CCS. Hospital, B. E.F., October 11, 1918. Dropped from rolls, November 8, 1918.

Curtiss, 19735, Herbert F, Sgt. On detached service at 3rd Instruction Centre for training as pilot.

Davis, 19847, Sherman D. Pvt.

Day, 19848, Harry Pvt. 1st Cl..

De Angelis, 388791, Andrew Pvt. Transferred to squadron from II Corps Replacement Battalion, October 6, 1918.

Decker, 19747, George Pvt.

Derrevere, 402473, Edward A. Pvt. Transferred to squadron from II Corps Replacement Battalion, October 6, 1918.

Devol, 19740, Lloyd E. Pvt.

Digman, 19729, Jesse A. Cpl.

D'Olic, 19749, Edward Pvt. Admitted to No. 9 General Hospital, B.E.F., May 1,1918. Dropped from rolls, Sept. 24, 1918.

Doloff, 1158058, Rudie D. Pvt. Transferred to squadron from II Corps Replacement Battalion, October 6, 1918.

Doty, 19849, Donald F. Pvt.

Douglass, 19775, Cecil N. Sgt. 1st Cl.

Douglass, 19773, John B. M.S.E.

Ellerkamp, 19798, Harry M. Cpl.

Ellis, 19703, William A. Pvt. 1st Cl.

Erdman, 19828, George B. Sgt.

E. Falkenstein, 19825, Howard W. Sgt.

Feigh, 19787, Glenn H Sgt.

Fellay, 19687, Dean R. Sgt.

Fellay, 19689, George R. Sgt. 1st Cl.

Ferris, 19850, Huber C. Cook

Fisher, 19800, Ben E. Pvt. 1st Cl.

Fleahman, 19778, William R. Cpl.

Floistad, 19751, Charles Pvt. Admitted to No. 55 C.C.S., B.E.F., May 25, 1918. Dropped from rolls, Sept. 23, 1918.

Foster, 19821, Roy B. Sgt. 1st Cl. Admitted to No. 55 U.S. General Hospital, November 21, 1918. Dropped from rolls, November 23, 1918.

Frater, 19801, John K. Cook

Gable, 19752, William J, Chauf. Admitted to No. 87 General Hospital, November 18, 1918. Dropped from rolls, November 23, 1918.

Galloway, 19731, Edward E. Sgt.

Gardner, 19693, Earl W. Cpl.

Garrett, 19779, Robert H. Chauf.

Gillman, 19851, Elmer H. Pvt.

Gipner, 19725, Lomas Sgt. 1st Cl.

Gnagy, 19852, John G. Chauf. 1st Cl.

Gosney, 19799, Howard M. Pvt. 1st Cl.

Green, 881054, Dallas W. Private Transferred to squadron from H Corps Replacement Battalion, October 6, 1918.

Guhm, 19780, Louis R. Cpl. Admitted to No. 6 Field Ambulance, St. Jean Hospital, October 29, 1918. Dropped from rolls, November 8, 1918.

Haley, 19853, Ralph E. Pvt.

Hardin, 2693209, Clarence W. Pvt. Transferred to squadron from H Corps Replacement Battalion, October 6, 1918.

Hathaway, 19594, Glenn S. Sgt. On detached service to 3rd Instruction Center training as pilot.

Heim, 19803, Anthony J. Pvt. 1st. Cl.

Herbsleb, 19753, George R. Cpl.

Hill, 19704, Reginald E. Pvt.

Hively, 19736, Eldon E. Sgt. 1st CI.

Hively, 19730, Roy H. Sgt. 1st CI.

Hollinger, 1052146, Harry E. Pvt. Transferred to squadron from II Corps Replacement Battalion, October 6, 1918.

Hollis, 19795, Everett R. Pvt. 1st Cl. Admitted to No. 30 General Hospital, July 28, 1918. Dropped from rolls September 13, 1918.

Holmes, 19822, Walter W. Sgt. 1st Cl.

Holton, 19803, Judson N. Pvt. Admitted to 3rd Australian Hospital, March 2, 1918. Dropped from rolls, September 23, 1918.

Horst, 19754, Frank H. Pvt. 1st Cl.

Huntington, 19781, Lester H. Cpl.

Irwin, 19854, Max A. Pvt. 1st Cl.

Jensen, 19837, Edwin R. Pvt. 1st Cl.

Johns, 19726, Leland H. Cpl.

Johnson, 19685, Alvin M. Mess Sgt.

Johnson, 19755, Archie Pvt. Transferred from squadron to Reclassification Barracks, October 24, 1918.

Johnson, 19760, Edwin L. Pvt.

Johnston, 19804, Adam B. Chauf.

Johnston, 19782, Logan T. Sgt.

Joplin, —— Edward R. Pvt. 1st Cl.

Karl, 19805, Frank J. Pvt. 1st Cl.

Kellum, 19833, Hayden C. Sgt. 1st Cl.

Kenney, 19788, John J. Pvt. 1st Cl.

King, 19756, Clark H. Pvt.

Knous, 19806, Alfred L. Cpl.

Kolb, 19705, John K. Pvt. 1st Cl.

Koop, 19699, Lamonte P. Cpl.

Lastovica, 19757, Frank R. Pvt. 1st Cl.

Latour, 19757, Oliver P. Pvt. Transferred to Reclassification Barracks, October 24, 1918.

Laughery, 19789, William A. Cpl.

Loughlin, 19907, Edward J. Pvt.

Leary, 19758, Carroll E. Pvt.

Lehr, 19688, Louis A. Chauf. 1st Cl.

Lemons, 19759, Lonnie Pvt.

Leonard, 19732, Lial W. Pvt. 1st Cl.

Leppin, 19808, Norman Chauf.

Ley, 19855, Arthur M. Pvt.

Long, 19809, Wallace B. Pvt.

Love, 19761, Virgil L. Pvt.

Malloy, 19762, Louis A. Pvt. Admitted to No. 21 C.C.S., August 26, 191 8. Dropped from rolls, October 24, 1918.

Martel, 19763, Clarence A. Pvt.

Masters, 19810, William H. Pvt.

McBride, 19764, Ralph C. Pvt.

McCarthy, 19800, Neal L Pvt. 1st Cl.

McPherson, 19811 , William F. Chauf.

Meek, Jr., 19856, James W. Pvt. 1st Cl.

Miller, 19812, Arthur F. Pvt.

Miller, 19776, Beryl O. Sgt.

Miller, 19784, Hayes R. Sgt. 1st Cl.

Miller, 1983 1, Henry T. Pvt.

Miller, 19696, Virgil L. Pvt.

Minehart, 19757, Arthur L. Cpl.

Mitchell, 19689, David S. Sgt. 1st Cl.

Morin, 19707, Fred P. Pvt.

Mueller, 19858, Louis E. Pvt.

Nelson, 19826, Harold W. Sgt.

O'Keefe, 19708, John J. Pvt.

Oldfield, 19709, Clyde S. Pvt. 1st Cl. Admitted to No. 6 Field Ambulance St. Jean Hospital, October 29, 1918. Dropped from rolls, November 8, 1918.

Oyster, 19859, Byron M. Chauf.

Parker, 19710, Edward L. Pvt.

Passerine, 3521 1, Emil E. Pvt. 1st Cl.

Pease, 252360, Tod H. Sgt. 1st Cl. Transferred to squadron from 183rd Flight Detachment. September 15, 1918.

Pendleton, 19765, Philip W. Pvt. Admitted to No 21 CCS. Hospital, B. E.F., August 19, 1918. Dropped from rolls, November 8, 1918.

Pickett, 19711, Sidney G. Pvt. Transferred to Reclassification Barracks, October 24, 1918.

Pollucci, 1062034, Nicholas J. Pvt. Transferred to squadron from II Corps Replacement Battalion, October 6, 1918.

Portugal, 19838, Harold W. Cpl. Admitted to hospital, August 5, 1918. Dropped from rolls, September 24, 1918.

Price, 19712, Sidney E. Pvt. 1st Cl.

Race, 369774, Homer H. Pvt. Transferred to squadron from II Corps Replacement Battalion, October 6, 1918.

Rader, 35212, George A. Pvt. Admitted to hospital August 18, 1918. Dropped from rolls, September 24, 1918.

Randolph, 34213, Frank B. Cpl.

Ransdell, 19791, Clarence T. Pvt. 1st Cl.

Ratzsch, 19795, Emerson R. Pvt. 1st Cl.

Reed, ——— William H. Cpl.

Reid, 1061152, William Pvt. Transferred to squadron from II Corps Replacement, Battalion, October 6, 1918.

Reilly, 19763, James F. Pvt.

Richman, 19815, Willie Pvt.

Rigby, 1067610, Edward Sgt. Transferred to squadron from II Corps Replacement Battalion, October 6, 1918.

Rose, 19767, Barton H. Pvt.

Rose, 19814, Halla E. Pvt. 1st Cl.

Ross, 19785, Jess Pvt. 1st Cl.

Routt, 1 97 1 4, Walter Pvt.

Sanford, 19733, Jay F. Sgt.

Seney, 19778, Leroy W. Pvt.

Slevin, 1 97 1 4, James J. Cpl.

Sloan, 19777, De Villo Sgt. 1st Cl.

Slover, 19839, George W. Pvt. 1st Cl. Admitted to No. 22 CCS. Hospital, B. E.F., October 8, 191 8. Dropped from rolls, October 24, 1918.

Smith, 19820, Cameron A. Sgt. 1st Cl.

Smith, 1 97 1 5, John G. Pvt. 1st Cl.

Speth, 19832, Roy H. Pvt. A.W.O.L., November 3, 1918. Dropped from rolls, November 23, 1918.

Spurling, 19816, Ernest E. Pvt.

Stephens, 19717, Harry B. Cpl. Admitted to No. 21 CCS. Hospital, October 11, 1918. Dropped from rolls, November 8, 1918.

Stickney, 198 16, Brune T. Pvt.

Stover, 1062266, Homer B. Pvt. Transferred to squadron from H Corps Replacement Battalion, October 6, 1918.

Strain, 19841, Fred Pvt. 1st Cl. Admitted to U.S. Base Hospital, Portsmouth, June 14, 1918. Dropped from rolls, September 24, 1918.

Strickland, 19786, Nelson J. Chauf.

Tanant, 2070092, James Pvt. Transferred to squadron from II Corps Replacement Battalion, October 6, 1918.

Tero, 19718, David H. Pvt. 1st Cl.

Thole, 35214, John G. Cpl.

Thompson, 19793, Blair M. Pvt. 1st Cl.

Thuman, 34215, George J. Pvt.

Thurman, 19860, Earl G. Pvt.

Toms, 19769, Cedric D. Pvt.

Traxler, 19770, Harry D. Pvt. 1st Cl.

Trezise, 198 18, Roy W. Chauf. 1st Cl.

Tyrrell, 19728, Hubert J. Pvt. 1st Cl.

Urquhart, 197 19, Davis L. Chauf.

Van Housen, 19734, Chester E. Cook

Wallace, 19774, Clyde B. Pvt. Transferred to Reclassification Barracks, October 30, 1918.

Waterland, 1058994, Gustav A. Pvt. Transferred to squadron from II Corps Replacement Battalion, October 6, 1918.

Wellborn, 19824, Clay A. Sgt. 1st Cl. Admitted to No. 45 Base

Hospital, Toul, November 19, 1918. Dropped from rolls, November 23, 1918.

Wessels, 19720, Clarence Cpl.

Whiteaker, 19792, William C. Pvt. 1st Cl.

Wilcavage, 19721, John Chauf. 1st Cl.

Wiley, 35216, Samuel C. Pvt. 1st Cl.

Willms, 19887, Clarence L. Cook

Wilson, 19771, Herbert D. Pvt. Transferred to Reclassification Barracks, October 30, 1918.

Wilson, 19830, Walter McC. Chauf. 1st Cl.

Winchester, 19722, Harry M. Chauf.

Wood, 19833, Lawrence C. Cpl.

Wray, 19723, Harold O. Cpl.

Wright, 288485, Gail H. Sgt. Transferred to squadron from 142nd Aero Squadron, July 4, 1918.

Young, 19819, Harold E. Cpl.

Zoubeck, 19784, Frank J. Sgt.

Attached (Medical Corps)

Haig, 640354, Alfred V. Pvt. 1st Cl. Attached to Squadron, July 4. 1918.

| | |
|---|---|
| Hartin, 643169, James Pvt. 1st Cl. | *ditto* |
| Homewood, 7 128 17, Arthur R. Sgt. | *ditto* |
| Schultz, 640386, Gardner S. Pvt. 1st Cl. | *ditto* |
| Statler, 640477, Donald P. Pvt. 1st Cl. | *ditto* |